# New Mexico's Book World

# New Mexico's
# BOOK WORLD
## A RESOURCE GUIDE

Complied by the members of the
New Mexico Book Association

Richard Polese, general editor

Sally Blakemore, design & graphics coordinator

Kathleen Sparkes, design & typography

**New Mexico Book Association**
Santa Fe, New Mexico

Although the editors have made every effort to provide current and accurate information, NMBA cannot assume responsibility for material provided to us. We regret any omissions or errors, and ask our readers to please inform us of any corrections and additions to be included in future editions.

*For additional copies, send a check or money order for $8.95 to: NMBA, P.O. Box 1295, Santa Fe, NM 87504.*

Copyright ©1997 New Mexico Book Association
All rights reserved. Printed in the United States of America.

Cover illustration by Sally Blakemore

FIRST EDITION

Published by:
**New Mexico Book Association**
Post Office Box 1295
Santa Fe, NM 87504
(505) 983-1412

Available to the book trade through:
**Ocean Tree Books**
1325 Cerro Gordo Road
Post Office Box 1295
Santa Fe, NM 87504

ISBN: 0-943734-33-9

Library of Congress Cataloging in Publication data:

**New Mexico's Book World:** a resource guide / compiled by members of the New Mexico Book Association : Richard Polese, general editor.
       p.    cm. — (New Mexico Book Association series)
   ISBN 0-943734-33-9
   1. Book industries and trade—New Mexico—Directories.
2. Libraries—New Mexico—Directories. I. Polese, Richard
II. New Mexico Book Association. III. Series.
Z478.3.N6N48     1996
381'.45002'025789—dc21               96-43527
                                         CIP

# Contents

Introduction . . . . . . . . . . . . . . . . . . . . . . . . . . . . . . . . . . . . . . . . 7

Memoirs of a New Mexico Bookman *by Robert F. Kadlec* . . . . . . . . 9

Introducing the New Mexico Book Association . . . . . . . . . . . . . . 12

**1** **New Mexico Book Association Members** . . . . . . . . . . . . . . . . . . 15

**2** **Book Publishers in New Mexico** . . . . . . . . . . . . . . . . . . . . . . . . . 35

**3** **Book Related Organizations** . . . . . . . . . . . . . . . . . . . . . . . . . . . . 48

**4** **Booksellers in New Mexico** . . . . . . . . . . . . . . . . . . . . . . . . . . . . . 53
   Independent Bookstores . . . . . . . . . . . . . . . . . . . . . . . . . . . . . . 54
   Antiquarians . . . . . . . . . . . . . . . . . . . . . . . . . . . . . . . . . . . . . . . 64
   Christian Bookstores . . . . . . . . . . . . . . . . . . . . . . . . . . . . . . . . . 66
   National Chain Stores . . . . . . . . . . . . . . . . . . . . . . . . . . . . . . . . 68
   Mail Order Services . . . . . . . . . . . . . . . . . . . . . . . . . . . . . . . . . 70
   Institutions (Colleges & Museums) . . . . . . . . . . . . . . . . . . . . . . 72

**5** **Distributors and Wholesalers** . . . . . . . . . . . . . . . . . . . . . . . . . . 79

**6** **Libraries in New Mexico** . . . . . . . . . . . . . . . . . . . . . . . . . . . . . . 82

**7** **Literacy Programs** . . . . . . . . . . . . . . . . . . . . . . . . . . . . . . . . . . . 97

**8** **Periodicals in New Mexico** . . . . . . . . . . . . . . . . . . . . . . . . . . . 106
   Newspapers . . . . . . . . . . . . . . . . . . . . . . . . . . . . . . . . . . . . . . 107
   Magazines . . . . . . . . . . . . . . . . . . . . . . . . . . . . . . . . . . . . . . . 110

**9** **Printers** . . . . . . . . . . . . . . . . . . . . . . . . . . . . . . . . . . . . . . . . . . 116
   New Mexico Printers . . . . . . . . . . . . . . . . . . . . . . . . . . . . . . . 117
   Out of State Book Printers . . . . . . . . . . . . . . . . . . . . . . . . . . . 123
   New Mexico Bookbinders . . . . . . . . . . . . . . . . . . . . . . . . . . . 126

**10** **Publishing Services** . . . . . . . . . . . . . . . . . . . . . . . . . . . . . . . . . 127
   Design, Prepress, and Graphic Services . . . . . . . . . . . . . . . . . . 128
   Editors and Indexers . . . . . . . . . . . . . . . . . . . . . . . . . . . . . . . 137
   Literary Agents . . . . . . . . . . . . . . . . . . . . . . . . . . . . . . . . . . . 139
   Marketing Services . . . . . . . . . . . . . . . . . . . . . . . . . . . . . . . . 139

Illustration Credits . . . . . . . . . . . . . . . . . . . . . . . . . . . . . . . . . 141

How to Join NMBA . . . . . . . . . . . . . . . . . . . . . . . . . . . . . . . . 143

## Acknowledgements

Many people cooperated to put together this first edition of *New Mexico's Book World*. We especially appreciate the contributions of Elizabeth Allred, Sara Benjamin-Rhodes, John Cole, Elaine Pinkerton Coleman, Robyn Covelli-Hunt, Cindy Goldenberg, Margaret Griffin, Marcy Heller, Edy Keeler, Barbara Beasley Murphy, Jaye Oliver, Paul Rhetts, Ann Racuya-Robbins, Harish C. Sharma, Debbie Starr, Jeanie C. Williams, Elizabeth Wolf, Richard Harris of PEN New Mexico, Karen Watkins of the New Mexico State Library, Kathy Flanary and Virginia Seiser of the New Mexico Library Association, and Michelle Jaschke and Rena Paradis of the New Mexico Coalition for Literacy.

*This first edition is dedicated to Dwight Myers, John Allred and Riley Parker, admired by book lovers throughout New Mexico for their devotion to the state's literary legacy.*

# Introduction

**W**elcome to the first edition of **New Mexico's Book World**—
the networking and information resource for the entire book
community of America's fifth largest—and arguably most
enchanting—state.

A place of writers, poets, and readers for centuries (Perez de
Villagra's *Historia de la Nueva Mexico* appeared in the mid-1500s),
New Mexico has experienced an explosion of publishing ferment
in the past dozen or so years. The number of new presses, particularly in Santa Fe and Albuquerque, seems at times to increase on
an almost daily basis, although new and interesting operations
have come into being in places such as Dexter, Angel Fire and El
Rito, far from the urban centers. In just the past three years, book
people in the state saw the birth of the New Mexico Book
Association, the Southwest Literary Center, and the New Mexico
Center for the Book, joining special interest groups as diverse as
the World Poetry Bout Association and the New Mexico Library
Association.

*New Mexico's Book World* was created by members of the New
Mexico Book Association to provide access to the many resources
now available and to build bridges between the hundreds of people for whom books and information are major parts of their professional and personal lives.

In each of the ten sections, you will find alphabetical listings
that include the mailing address, phone, fax and e-mail numbers,
and often the principal person to contact. In the list of NMBA
members, which appears first, you will find a description of the
business, profession or service of nearly everyone (membership
has its privileges!). When the task of finding every published
author or listing every K-8 school library in the state seemed
overwhelming, we decided instead to include the names and
addresses of organizations that can provide such information.

As soon as a resource such as this is published it begins to become obsolete. We need your help making sure that information is correct and up-to-date. And we realize that in a first effort such as this errors and omissions inevitably occur. We apologize for these, and will do our best to rectify them in future editions. If you find an error, omission, or someone new who should be included, please contact NMBA.

We are open to suggestions for new categories and format changes that will help make this an even more useful resource for everyone. Meanwhile, we hope that *New Mexico's Book World* will become your dog-eared, dependable companion!

—*Richard Polese*

# Memoirs of a New Mexico Bookman

## By Robert F. Kadlec

*Robert Kadlec is one of New Mexico's legendary elder bookmen. His appearance in Santa Fe from Chicago spanned the end of an older era of bookselling and publishing here and the less-whimsical (and more frenetic) modern renaissance. He was proprietor of the Ancient City Bookshop in Sena Plaza in the 1960s, and continues to deal in used and rare Southwest Americana through the mail under the name Abacus Books.* —Richard Polese

**W**hen I arrived in Santa Fe in 1949, one of my first orders of business was to contact local publishers and printers. At the time there were six or seven listed in the phone book and I visited each one to determine how they might fit into my forthcoming business venture.

All of them had the then-basic printing press, Multigraph, paper cutter, and other equipment with which to produce the finished product—a bound book. Most could manage a book with paper covers, but the *New Mexican*, the city's daily newspaper of long standing, had all the equipment needed to produce a cloth-covered book. Over the years, the *New Mexican* not only printed the newspaper but turned out a large number of titles. Southwestern Publishing Company was a general publisher for many years, in business on West Palace Avenue and Burro Alley. It was established by Richard Bokum and offered a variety of general printing services. About 25 years ago the building burned. Bokum cleared the area and built the present three-story business building which stands on the site today. I don't recall if Bokum ever went back into publishing.

Schifani Brothers operated a publishing and printing venture on Marcy Street, next door to the *New Mexican*, publishing some books and doing job printing. Their physical plant was quite adequate and as a result they were able to produce a fine product. Schifani Brothers continues in business today in modern quarters at 502 Cerrillos Road.

Graphic Printing Company was in a building adjacent to the living quarters of its owners, Barbara and Frank Vergara, in the 200 block of Washington Avenue. They were publishers of a number of titles, taking special care to turn out exceptionally good work. Soon after their opening, a fire started in the plant and destroyed much of their paper stock, furnishings and anything else that would burn. I knew Barbara and Frank from earlier years and spent a couple of days helping in the cleanup. The business then continued under the name Vergara Printing Company, moving much later to quarters on Airport Road.

C. B. Mayshark Lithographing had a small printery on Hickox Street and published a few pamphlets. And a Mr. Naranjo printed and published numerous pamphlets in Spanish and English, but this little shop did not stay in business long.

Rufus Graves owned several old presses and produced booklets about Santa Fe events. Also in that era, Dorothy Stewart, sister of the owner of Canyon Road's El Zaguan complex, put out some small society publications on what was likely a Chandler and Price press.

Rydal Press had relocated from Tesuque and was set up on Canyon Road when I arrived. Walter Goodwin started the press in Rydal, Pennsylvania in 1933 and moved to New Mexico about two years later. In the early 1950s, Gordon Stevenson was president of Rydal and Dale Bullock was vice-president and general manager at Rydal. They produced many fine and interesting books and did job printing, including window display cards, booklet-type programs for events such as rodeos, horse shows, etc. In fact, they printed just about anything anyone needed. Bullock was known to his customers as Pappy, a name he really didn't care about, but accepted since it was bestowed by his wife Alice, who became known for her writings on New Mexico history. After Bullock's death, Rydal passed through other hands. Although no longer at the Canyon Road location and long since out of the job printing business, Rydal carries on today as a chapbook publisher under Clark Kimball.

Mary and Charles Comfort published a few pamphlets and ventured into a weekly magazine called *The Santa Fe Scene*, which was published in a 5¹/₂" by 8" format for a number of years.

Jack Rittenhouse and his wonderful Stagecoach Press came along in the early 1960s. He hand-printed small hard cover limited editions of very high aesthetic and literary value about Southwestern subjects—but that's another story!

The State of New Mexico must be considered as a major local publisher. Through its various departments it has published many books and booklets over the years on a variety of state-related subjects. *New Mexico Magazine* began as the *New Mexico Highway Journal* sometime in the early 1920s.

There may be others, of course, whose names and faces in a time-lapse of many decades elude me, but they were all publishers as defined by Noah Webster: **publisher**—*one who publishes, especially one who issues, or causes to be issued, from the press and offers for sale or circulation, printed matter, engraved, or the like.*

# Introducing the NMBA

**T**wo seemingly unrelated events led to the creation of the New Mexico Book Association in April 1994. For several years, New Mexico members of the Rocky Mountain Book Publishers Association, which was founded here, met for lunch on the first Friday of the month to share news and friendship and network informally. RMBPA had grown strongly over the years; a succession of its executive directors were based in Colorado, and meanwhile in New Mexico the publishing community was booming. Moreover, the Friday luncheons were starting to draw people whose weren't just publishers, but included writers, editors, illustrators, designers, and bookstore owners.

Early that year, word spread that the Feria Internacional del Libro (better known as the Guadalajara Book Fair), the premier Spanish language book event in the world, had selected New Mexico as the featured theme for the 1994 fair. This was the first time a political unit other than a nation had been chosen. It was quite an honor, but how were we going to represent the state properly? Victor di Suvero and Michael O'Shaughnessy met with people from the local RMBPA group and suggested a new association to serve as the parent for a Guadalajara-New Mexico Task Force. The founding members of New Mexico Book Publishers Association were Ancient City Press (Mary Powell), Clear Light Publishers (Harmon Houghton), Museum of New Mexico Press (Ron Lattimer, Greg Wright), Ocean Tree Books (Richard Polese), Pennywhistle Press (di Suvero) and Red Crane Books (O'Shaughnessy and his wife Marianne). Other publishers quickly joined the fold and our presence at Guadalajara was a success.

But now Guadalajara was behind us, a new association was in place, and the luncheons were more popular than ever. Recognizing that our common interests went beyond just publishing, we dropped the word Publisher from our name, opened membership to all people interested in the Book in New Mexico, and created the *Libro* newsletter. Paul Rhetts of LPD Press brought out the first *Libro* in March 1995 in a lively and useful format.

NMBA has taken part in public and professional events such as the New Mexico Library Association conference in Las Cruces and the Libros Book Fair in Santa Fe. We hold an annual membership meeting and election of directors in the spring. We are taking an active interest in economic opportunities for members, finding ways to involve and mentor young people, and have put together *New Mexico's Book World: A Resource Guide*. We meet now not only in Santa Fe, but also have occasional dinner meetings in Albuquerque. Along with other major regional book groups, we have a sister relationship with RMBPA. And this past year NMBA board member Marianne O'Shaughnessy worked with other members and literary and library groups to give birth to the New Mexico Center for the Book.

NMBA has a home page on the internet, created for us in cooperation with Webworks of Santa Fe:

**www.roadrunner.com/~webworks/nmba**

You'll find complete information about our members and services, and the first page of the current Libro. Our e-mail address is: **nmba@roadrunner.com**

Membership is by individual, and even those who live out of state can join — the only criteria is an interest in the Book in New Mexico. Our membership year runs September through September. If you'd like to join us, and we hope you will, you'll find a membership form at the back of *New Mexico's Book World*.

> **Richard Polese,** *president*
> **Ann Racuya-Robbins,** *vice president*
> **Jeanie C. Williams,** *secretary*
> **Barbara Beasley Murphy,** *treasurer*
> **Elizabeth Allred,** *director*
> **Sally Blakemore,** *director*
> **Elaine Pinkerton Coleman,** *director*
> **Robyn Covelli-Hunt,** *director*
> **Harmon Houghton,** *director*
> **Sara Benjamin-Rhodes,** Libro *editor*

# New Mexico Book Association

## MISSION STATEMENT

**TO PRESERVE** and perpetuate the Book (in the broadest sense of the term, including magazines and other printed manifestations of the written word and photographs) as a repository of the wisdom of the past, the essence of the present and a guide to the future.

**TO WORK** with all interested individuals as well as all professionals involved in the production, manufacture, publication, distribution and sales of books so as to enhance public recognition and appreciation of books written by New Mexico authors, dealing with New Mexico issues, or produced or published in New Mexico.

**TO SUPPORT** and work with all organizations and associations, both public and private, interested in the promotion of the Book itself, of literacy in general and of educational resources designed to serve the widest public possible.

**IN THIS DAY** and age, when the intrusion and expansion of television and the other media in the daily life of our citizenry is reaching previously unimagined levels, Books and Book publishing are experiencing a profound transformation.

**THE MEMBERS** of the New Mexico Book Association pledge their best efforts, in a spirit of cooperation and trust, to work with all other demonstrably dedicated persons to maintain, promote and perpetuate the Book as an essential element of our lives, our histories and our function as responsible citizens.

## 1994 – 1997

# New Mexico Book Association Members

**NMBA** is the professional and trade fraternity of the men and women who either work in the world of books or are New Mexico people for whom books are an abiding passion. Membership is by individual, and all members as of September 1996 are listed here alphabetically.

These listings include the names of the firms or institutions our members are associated with, plus a brief description of their activities. Look also in the other sections of this book (Book Publishers, Organizations, Publishing Services, etc.) for more about how NMBA people are involved in New Mexico's world of books. To join NMBA, return the Membership Form at the back of *New Mexico's Book World*.

### Victoria Agee

*Agee Indexing Services*
7436 El Morro Rd NE
Albuquerque, NM 87109
505-823-2306
f: 505-823-2306
e-mail: keeg55c@aol.com

Over 20 years experience in periodical, book and archival indexing for numerous clients including Library of Congress, Congressional Quarterly, and the New Mexico Magazine. Also provide index design, bibliography preparation and cataloging services.

### Becky Allison

*Gilliland Printing, Inc.*
215 N. Summit
Arkansas City, KS 67005
800-332-8200
   316-442-0500
   f: 316-442-8504

*Gilliland Printing* specializes in printing perfectbound book runs from 500 to 20,000. We offer competitive pricing, 24 hour estimates, 10-20 working day turn times, full typesetting & design work, disk-to-film capabilities and first-class customer service.

### Elizabeth Allred

*Exceptional Books, Ltd.*
798 47th St
Los Alamos, NM 87544
505-662-6601
f: 505-662-6601
103576,1336@compuserve.com

We are an eclectic small publisher tending to history and legend, but willing to look at other topics.

### Janeal Arison

*A+ Productions*
PO Box 2444
Santa Fe, NM 87504
505-988-4434
f: 505-989-1030

*A+ Productions* is dedicated to the production of Suki stories, a series of career role modeling books for all girls. The books encourage girls to use their imagination, explore possibilities and believe in themselves. Arison's business partner is Nancy Avedisian.

### Judith Asher

*Sherman Asher Publishing*
PO Box 2853
Santa Fe, NM 87504
505-984-2686
f: 505-820-2744
PoetJudith@aol.com

*Sherman Asher Publishing* is a small press dedicated to the rhythms of adventure and has already shifted to the new paradigm. Front line reports are available as poetry, non-fiction and CD-ROMs.

### Nancy S. Avedisian

*A+ Productions*
2021 Conejo Dr.
Santa Fe, NM 87505
505-988-4434
f: 505-988-4434

Freelance editing, proofreading, indexing with "relentless devotion to the written word."

### Cindy Barrilleaux

150 Skyland
Tijeras, NM 87509
505-281-7737

## Catherine Baudoin

*Maxwell Museum Store*
University of New Mexico
Albuquerque, NM 87131
505-277-8601, 277-3700

## George Donoho Bayless

*Donoho Books*
PO Box 804
El Rito, NM 87530
505-581-4574
f: 505-573-7700

Donoho Books is named after my great-great grandmother, *Mary Donoho–New First Lady of the Santa Fe Trail* (Ancient City Press, 1991), Marian Meyer's book about the first white woman in New Mexico, 1833.

## Oliver Beaudette

*Heartsfire Books*
500 N. Guadalupe St
Suite G-465
Santa Fe, NM 87501
505-988-5160
f: 505-986-1781
e-mail: spiritroad@aol.com

Heartsfire Books, an imprint of *Hampton Roads Publishing*, publishes stories of people who are following spirit in their journeys and have meditations, exercises or techniques that others may find helpful on their own paths of discovery.

## Sara Benjamin-Rhodes

*Sovereignty Press*
PO Box 6095
Santa Fe, NM 87502
505-466-6975
f: 505-466-0887
e-mail:
  sovpress@internetMCI.com

Full production services for publishers and self-publishers: edit-

ing, typography, graphics, layout, design, from manuscript through electronic prepress. Experienced, professional, with outstanding references. Call for free brochure or consultation. The *best* costs no more!

## James Berry

*The Message Company*
4 Camino Azul
Santa Fe, NM 87505
505-474-0998
f: 505 471 2584

Publisher specializing in new energy, new science, freedom and new business paradigms. Produces books, audio and video tapes and other media.

## Sallie Bingham

69 Montezuma #316
Santa Fe, NM 87501
505-989-1205

Novelist and playwright (seven books published). Next: a novel, *Straight Man* (Fall, 1996)

## Jenifer Blakemore

*Editorial Services*
809 Gonzales Rd
Santa Fe, NM 87501
505-820-7713
f: 505-820-0800

Editorial services: editor, copy editor, and indexer. Because "Words are very rascals."
— William Shakespeare, *Twelfth Night* (III.i.20)

## Sally Blakemore

*Arroyo Projects Studio*
Fortaleza Coyote
1413 Second St, 2nd floor
Santa Fe, NM 87501
505-988-2331
f: 505-988-2164

*Arroyo Projects Studio* packages unusual novelty books and products for national and international publishers and other markets. We provide complete design, paper engineering, and print production services. Sally is the creative director. Her partners is Edy Keeler, marketing director.

## Dianne Borneman

*Shadow Canyon Graphics*
PO Box 2765
2276 Pebble Beach Ct
Evergreen, CO 80439
303-670-0401
f: 303-670-0401

Book design and typography, page composition, cover and jacket design, editorial and indexing services.

## Karen Bowden

1925 Spinorlet Drive
La Jolla, CA 92037
619-454-8594
f: 619-454-3626

## Fern Brucker

1073 Abbey Lane
Española, NM 87532
505-753-5636
f: 505-989-8608
e-mail:
    jpbruck@roadrunner.com

Consultant to publishing in the educational field.

## Nash Candelaria

111 E. San Mateo Rd
Santa Fe, NM 87505
505-983-0795

Novelist and short story writer about Hispanic New Mexico, focusing on cultural and generational conflicts. Work described as landmarks of Hispanic literature. Recipient of The Before Columbus Foundation American Book Award.

## Steven Cary

*John Muir Publications*
PO Box 613
Santa Fe, NM 87504
505-982-4078
f: 505-988-1680

Publishing books in Santa Fe since 1969. Currently issuing 60 books per year with main focus in travel and juvenile non-fiction. JMP has 18 employees and engages many independent editors and graphic artists.

## Regina Chavez

*Hispanic Culture Foundation*
PO Box 7279
Albuquerque, NM 87194
505-831-8360

## Ronald Christ

*Lumen, Inc.*
40 Camino Cielo
Santa Fe, NM 87501
505-988-5820
voice & f: 505-988-9236
e-mail: site@rt66.com

*Lumen* is the online publisher of *Site Architecture* magazine, and print publisher of books on architecture and design. Also literary and literature translations from Spanish to English.

## Tom Claffey

PO Box 23332
Santa Fe, NM 87502
505-983-6738

Writer.

## John Cole

*John Cole Graphic Designer*
3 Juego Place
Santa Fe, NM 87505
505-466-7311
f: 505466-2624
e-mail: jcolegrahpic@aol.com

24 years in publishing, offering design meant to sell your product. Specializing in desktop capabilities. Software publisher: *GD Estimating 2.0* for graphic designers recently listed in *Macworld* magazine.

## Elaine Pinkerton Coleman

899 East Zia Rd
Santa Fe, NM 87505
505-983-9747
f: 505-983-0743
e-mail: elaine@trail.com

Elaine Pinkerton is the author of *Santa Fe On Foot* and *The Santa Fe Trail By Bicycle*. As a freelance journalist, she has published numerous travel articles. Available for technical writing, editing, and promotional work.

## Julie Conner

*Conner Design*
223 N. Guadalupe
Santa Fe, NM 87501
505-982-7895
f: 505-982-0908
e-mail:
    dzinmuz@unix.nets.com

## Robyn Covelli-Hunt

*Sun Publishing*
PO Box 5588
Santa Fe, NM 87502
505-471-5177
f: 505-473-4458

*Sun Publishing* specializes in reprinting metaphysical classics. Robyn has served as NMBA's secretary.

## John F. Crawford

*West End Press*
PO Box 27334
Albuquerque, NM 87125
505-345-5729
f: 505-345-5729

82 titles published, 24 active. Chiefly Southwestern small press publisher in business 20 years, ten in Albuquerque. Features Native American, Spanish/ Chicano, multicultural, women, political writing – poetry, fiction, drama.

## Francine Cronshaw

*East Mountain Editing Services*
PO Box 1895
Tijeras, NM 87059
w: 505-281-8422
f: 505-281-8422
e-mail: cronshaw@unm.edu

Indexing and copy-editing of Latin American content and bilingual editions, as well as general interest manuscripts. Trade, academic and government client base. Member of American Society of Indexers and American Historical Association. Spanish-to-English translations.

## Gene Crouch

*Buffalo Publications*
718 Baca St
Santa Fe, NM 87501
505-983-1226
f: 505-983-5256

25 years experience in the publications game. Editorial and production.

## Ron Cubelo

*Rose Printing Co.*
2503 Jackson Bluff Rd
Tallahassee, FL 32304
800-227-3725
f: 904-576-4153
e-mail:roseprt@freenet.fsu.edu

*Rose Printing* is a complete in-house book manufacturer specializing in short runs. Trim sizes from mini-books to 12"x19". In-house electronic prepress capabilities.

## Gladys Dana

*The Dana Book Store*
203 Manzanares St
Socorro, NM 87801
505-835-3434
800-524-3434

Independent bookstore featuring new books, children's room, large since fiction collection. Founded in 1981. Open 9am-9pm seven days a week. Located in the historic Val Verde Hotel, one block east of California Ave.

## Margaret Davenport

409 E. Palace Ave #7
Santa Fe, NM 87501
505-986-1114

## Victor di Suervo

*Pennywhistle Press*
PO Box 734
Tesuque, NM 87574
505-982-2622
f: 505-982-6858

*Pennywhistle Press* was started in 1989 as a way to present the work of notable poets to the reading public. Known for its Poetry Chapbook Series, the Press has recently expanded its offering of poetry to readers by branching out into the anthology market with the publication of *Saludos! Poemas de Nuevo Mexico*, a collection of 66 poets writing about the magical New Mexico way of life.

## James J. Dunlap

*Alla Bookstore*
102 W. San Francisco, St #20
Santa Fe, NM 87501
505-988-5416
f: 505-820-7048

Books of the Americas; Spanish & Portuguese language books.

## Antonio R. Garces

*Red Rabbit Press*
PO Box 6545
Santa Fe, NM 87502
505-982-1773

Publishes *Adobe Angels: The Ghost of Santa Fe and Taos*; *Adobe Angels: The Ghost of Albuquerque*; and *Adobe Angels: The Ghost of Las Cruces & Southern New Mexico*. Interviews of citizens' encounters with ghosts!

## Vernon J. Glover

*Southwest Specialties*
PO Box 4077
Manassas, VA 20108
703-257-7997

Railroads, mining, logging, Southwest business and industrial history, 1878-1970. Books, manuscripts, original research, synopses and indices of primary data from regional and national archives. Large personal information base. Occasional research to order.

## Alex Goulder

*Ripon Community Printers*
1919 Fourteenth St, Suite 540
Boulder, CO 80302
303-443-7884
f: 303-443-8288
goulder@earthnet.net

Ripon's Wisconsin plant specializes in high-quality, low-cost catalogs, magazines, and softcover books printed on state-of-the-art non-heatset webs. Complete printing services from digital prepress to mailing.

## Michael Hall

*Golden Heart Publications*
PO Box 6759
Santa Fe, NM 87502
505-466-0877

Hall's books, *Flight Lessons* and *Pioneer Journal*, have enjoyed worldwide recognition. His third book, *A Beginner's Guide to True Freedom*, is due in 1996.

## Kingsley Hammett

*Fleetwood Press*
2405 Maclovia Lane
Santa Fe, NM 87505
505-471-4599
f: 505-471-4549

*Fleetwood Press* publishes a series of books about New Mexico furniture which include plans and drawings to enable craftsmen to reproduce historic styles from over 400 years of craft history. Titles: *Classic New Mexican Furniture* and *Spanish Colonial Furniture of the WPA Period.*

## David Harlan

*Gilliland Printing*
76 Verano Loop
Santa Fe, NM 87505
505-466-3052

Representative for full-service book printer.

## Linda G. Harris

*Arroyo Press*
PO Box 4333
Las Cruces, NM 88003
505-522-2348
Orders: 800-795-2692

*Arroyo Press* features Southern New Mexico writers, photographers, and artists in books about the Southwest. *Arroyo Press* publishes cloth and quality paperback books on architecture, history, biography, travel, and fiction.

### Richard Harris

PEN New Mexico
2860 Plaza Verde
Santa Fe, NM 87505
505-988-5582

Richard Harris is president of PEN New Mexico, a statewide organization of published authors that fights censorship and supports freedom of expression. Activities include readings, networking, and professional development.

### Barbara Hart

New Mexico State University
  Library-Serial Receipts
Box 30006, Dept. 3475
Las Cruces, NM 88003

Academic research library serving the students and community of Las Cruces, New Mexico and Dona Ana County.

### Mark T. Hartman

Hartman Publishing Inc.
8529-A Indian School Rd NE
Albuquerque, NM 87112
505-291-1274
f: 505-291-1284

Hartman Publishing produces educational materials for the health care industries.

### Joe Hayes

Trails West Publishing
PO Box 8619
Santa Fe, NM 87504
505-982-8058
f: 915-566-9072

Trails West was formed by storyteller Joe Hayes to publish audio cassettes to accompany his books. Distributed by Cinco Puntos Press in El Paso.

### Margret Henkels

H. Margret Studio/Gallery
622-C Canyon Road
Santa Fe, NM 87501
505-989-8032

Book art and illustration.

### Nancy Hewitt

An Extra Hand
627 Gomez Road
Santa Fe, NM 87501
505-989-4119

Freelance print production supervisor: detail oriented, 25 years experience. Coordinate projects, concept to delivery, working with designers, writers, publishers and all outside suppliers. Knowledgeable all types of printing. Responsible for reproduction quality, estimating, cost control, deadlines.

### Jim Holefka

Thompson-Shore, Inc.
7300 West Joy Rd
Dexter, MI 48130
313-426-3939
f: 800-706-4545
e-mail: http://www.tshore.com

Thompson-Shore is a major short and medium run trade book printer, with state-of-the-art electronic prepress capabilities.

### Harmon Houghton

Clear Light Publishers
823 Don Diego
Santa Fe, NM 87501
505-989-9590
clpublish@aol.com

Publishes Native American and Western titles focusing on the art, culture and legacy of traditional lifestyles. The subject areas include art, biography, children's books, cookbooks, environmental, health and history. Please call for current catalog and full listing. Marcia Keegan is Harmon's partner.

## Dianne Howie

*Westcliffe Publishers, Inc.*
PO Box 1261
Englewood, CO 80150
303-935-0900
f: 303-935-0903

High-quality, four-color, regional nature photography books, guidebooks, cookbooks and wall/engagement calendars. Publishers of *Outside Magazine's* "Exposure" calendar and The Wilderness Society's "Wilderness" calendar. Featuring books and calendars by John Fielder.

## Paul E. Huntsberger

*Two Eagles Press, International*
PO Box 208
Las Cruces, NM 88004
505-523-7911
f: 505-523-1953
e-mail: pjhuntsber@aol.com

Publishers of books dealing with international or intercultural themes; designers of books, catalogs, technical reports, educational and training materials, and newsletters. (Formerly EDITTS... Publishing.)

## Michael Huston

*Quality Books, Inc.*
1003 W. Pines Rd
Oregon, IL 61061
815-732-4499

Library distributor. More than 32 years experience in the distribution of independently published books, special interest videos, and new multimedia to libraries.

## Betty John

10501 Lagrima de Oro NE, #338
Albuquerque, NM 87111
505-291-3338

## Edy Keeler

*Keeler Communication*
89 Apache Ridge
Santa Fe, NM 87505
505-466-4040
f: 505-466-8223

Marketing and publicity services for book people.

## Al Kelly

*Data Reproductions Corporation*
1480 N. Rochester Road
Rochester Hills, MI 48307
810-652-7600
f: 810-652-7605
datarep@ibm.net

Sales representative for Michigan book printer providing all binding styles. One and two color text printing from camera-ready copy or disk. Four color covers, jackets and inserts with lamination/ UV coating. Recycled paper.

## Ellen Kleiner

*Blessingway Authors' Services*
134 East Lupita Road
Santa Fe, NM 87505
505-983-2649
f: 505-983-2005
e-mail: blessingwy@aol

Full range of editorial, production, and consulting services for self-publishing authors, busy publishers, and writers seeking publication, including substantive editing, word processing, design, page composition, proofreading, book proposals, printer boards, marketing and publicity.

## Lisa Knudsen

*Mountains and Plains*
  *Booksellers Association*
805 LaPorte Avenue
Fort Collins, CO 80521
800-752-0249, 970-484-5856
f: 970-407-1479
e-mail: /knumpba@rmi.net

MPBA is a nonprofit trade association of booksellers, book wholesalers and publishers located throughout the Rocky Mountain Region. Formed more than 30 years ago, MPBA now numbers 450 members from eight states.

## Vi Kochendoerfer

226 North 60 Avenue East
  Duluth MN 55804
218-525-2006

Published author: *One Woman's World War II* (University Press, Kentucky), *A Modern Pioneer* (Skinner House, Boston). Now working on *Santa Fe in the Fifties*.

## Ronald Latimer

*Museum of New Mexico Press*
228 E. Palace Ave
PO Box 2087
Santa Fe, NM 87503
505-827-6454
f: 505-827-7308

Publishes general trade and art quality titles on the arts and cultures of the Southwest and beyond. Subjects include the fine and folk arts, Native American and Hispanic life, anthropology, history, and nature.

## Linda K. Lewis

*University of New Mexico*
  *General Libraries; Collections-*
  *Development Department*
Albuquerque, NM 87131
505-277-7828
f: 505-277-6019
llewis@unm.edu

The University of New Mexico General Library's Center for Southwest Research has strong collections in New Mexican history, literature and related areas.

## Maggie Lichtenberg

*Margaret Klee Lichtenberg*
  *& Associates*
PO Box 268
Santa Fe, NM 87504
505-986-8807
f: 505-986-8794
margaretkl@aol.com

Margaret Klee Lichtenberg, with 20 years of mainstream east coast publishing experience (Simon & Schuster, Bantam, Grove Press, Beacon Press), is a book marketing coach specializing in coaching authors, freelancers, small publishers, and self-publishers through the publishing, marketing, distribution, and subsidiary rights process.

## Mary Luders

434 Acequia Madre
Santa Fe, NM 87501
505-982-5302

Development editor, agent, publishing consultant. Thirteen years of book publishing experience, specializing in non-fiction, illustrated, series and novelty formats.

### James Mafchir

*Western Edge Press*
126 Candelario
Santa Fe, NM 87501
505-988-7214
f: 505-988-7214

Publishes quality books on Southwestern subjects. Design and production services with Quark capabilities. Color reproduction specialist.

### Wells Mahkee, Jr.

*Zuni A:shiwi Publishing*
PO Box 3007
Zuni, NM 87327
505-782-4880
f: 505-782-2136

*Zuni A:shiwi* Publishing produces quality books about the distinctive culture of Zuni, and by focusing on Zuni authors, from the unique Zuni perspective. *Zuni A:shiwi* presents fiction and nonfiction books for all ages.

### Carol Maness

*New Mexico State University Bookstore*
PO Box 30004, Dept. CC
Las Cruces, NM 88003
505-646-7660
f: 505-646-6022

### Erik J. Mason

*State House Press*
1882 Conejo Dr
Santa Fe, NM 87505
505-982-1258

Editor and factotum for *State House Press*, a small but prestigious Austin firm specializing in Texana and reprints of rare books but with three titles by James A. Michener.

### Christine Mather

Route 19 Box 88D
Santa Fe, NM 87505
505-988-1218

Published author non-fiction: *Santa Fe Style, Native America, True West, Santa Fe Christmas.* Extensive art history-museum background. Currently: museum projects, monthly "style" column, adolescent fiction.

### Janie Matson

*Yucca Tree Press*
2130 Hixon Dr
Las Cruces, NM 88005
505-524-2357

*Yucca Tree Press* specializes in Southwestern and military history, particularly of a regional nature. A new series was inaugurated with the December 1995 publication of *Only the Echoes: The Life of Howard Bass Cushing.* The series, entitled "Frontier People and Forts" will publish a book every 12-18 months, available in both paper and in a numbered and signed limited edition.

### Joel Mathews

*Tulane Exchange*
111 Tulane Dr SE
Albuquerque, NM 87108
505-260-0792

Used books and records.

## Kay Matthews

*Acequia Madre Press*
Box 6 El Valle Route
Chamisal, NM 87521
505-689-2200
f: 505-689-2200
e-mail: acequia@laplaza.org

*Acequia Madre Press* publishes regional outdoor guidebooks – hiking, backpacking and cross-country skiing – that include technical, historical and environmental information. We also publish books dealing with environmental issues for children and adults.

## Ronald Mazzola

*McNaughton & Gunn Inc.*
960 Woodland Drive
Saline, MI 48176
313-429-5411
f: 800-677-BOOK

Complete book printing services for perfect bound and case binding. Print runs from 250 copies to 25,000, on sheet-fed and web presses.

## Michael W. McCowen

*Capitan Publishing Co.*
PO Box 156
Dexter, NM 88230
505-354-4241

*Capitan Publishing Company* features New Mexico and Southwest historical fiction with stories infused with personal insights and self-expressive interpretations.

## Maurice R. McDonald

*Kiva Publishing, Inc.*
102 E. Water St
Santa Fe, NM 87501
505-820-7413

## Mary Dungan Megalli

PO Box 1375
El Prado, NM 87529
505-751-1184

Editing, typing, proofreading, including technical; international experience.

## Peter Michaelson

*Prospect Books*
PO Box 8362
Santa Fe, NM 87504
505-438-3732

*Prospect Books*, on the cutting edge of psychology and health, publishes titles that explore the hidden aspects of human nature, exposing the way we create our own failure and unhappiness. Books focus on personal growth and creative enhancement, and a radically new method that exposes root causes of self-limiting emotions and behaviors. The authors, Peter and Sandra Michaelson, are licensed psychotherapists with 20 years experience.

## Joe Mowrey

*Mariposa Printing & Publishing*
922 Baca St
Santa Fe, NM 87501
505-988-5582

## Barbara Beasley Murphy

486 Circle Drive
Santa Fe, NM 87501
505-983-9607

Author; published titles: *Fly Like an Eagle* (Delacorte & Dell Paper); *Ace Hits the Big Time*, (Dell); American Library Assn. List: *The Best 100 Books for Young Adults of Last 25 Years.*

## Barbara Myers

*Santa Fe Graphic Design*
PO Box 2507
Santa Fe, NM 87504
505-466-0816
f: 505-466-9788

Illustrator, graphic design; traditional and computer concepts.

## Carol Myers

*New Mexico Book League*
8632 Horacio Pl NE
Albuquerque, NM 87111
505-299-8940
f: 505-294-8032

The *New Mexico Book League* publishes *Book Talk*, the magazine for involved Southwestern bibliophiles for 25 years. We act in an advisory capacity for anyone with problems or questions regarding the world of books in the Southwest.

## Robert J. Nordhaus

64 Juniper Hill Loop NE
Albuquerque, NM 87122

Author.

## Colleen Olinger

*Otowi Station Bookstore/
Otowi Crossing Press*
1350 Central Ave
Los Alamos, NM 87544
505-662-9589, 505-455-2691
f: 505-455-7401

We are a combination general bookstore (specializing in atomic history, technical and children's books) and a science museum store. We also have a small publishing operation.

## Jaye Oliver

1600-B Brae Street
Santa Fe, NM 87505
505-820-7092

Jaye Oliver designs and illustrates books, catalogs and brochures. In business as a freelance artist since 1979, she recently settled in Santa Fe with new ideas for children's and special interest books.

## Marianne O'Shaughnessy

*Red Crane Books, Inc.*
2008 Rosina St, Suite B
Santa Fe, NM 87501
505-988-7070
f: 505-989-7476
e-mail:
    crane1@roadrunner.com

*Red Crane Books* is committed to publishing books that foster an understanding of human diversity. Our interest is in art, cooking, how-to, literature, social history, travel, and other areas that complement our list.

## Sandra Patterson

*Publishers Group West*
4287 Troutdale Village Dr
Evergreen, CO 80439
303-674-3772
f: 303-727-6215

PGW sales rep for New Mexico, Colorado, Utah, Montana and Wyoming.

## Patricia A. Pearce

*Delgado Street Studio*
110 Delgado St
Santa Fe, NM 87501
505-984-8901

Fine art instruction in print-making and hand-made art books.

## David G. Plumer

*Walsworth Publishing Co.*
1101 E. 101st Terrace, #100
Kansas City, MO 64131
*Headquarters:*
306 N. Kansas Ave
Marceline, MO 64658
800-369-2646
f: 816-258-7798

Quality short-run sheet-fed printer and binder specializing in four-color and halftone reproduction, casebound and soft cover books.

## Richard Polese

*Ocean Tree Books*
PO Box 1295
Santa Fe, NM 87504
505-983-1412
f: 505-983-1412
e-mail: oceantre@trail.com

*Ocean Tree Books*, founded in 1983, publishes "Adventure Roads Travel" guides to Southwestern and Southern states, and inspirational, peacemaking and local history titles. *Santa Fe On Foot* and *Peace Pilgrim's Wisdom* are two of our most popular titles. *From Santa Fe to O'Keeffe Country* appeared as a Fall, 1996 book.

## Nancy Pollack

*The Ansel Group*
3660 Cerrillos Rd, B-9
Santa Fe, NM 87505
505-473-5100
f: 505-473-9393

## Joseph Pomerance

*Editorial Services*
215 St. John's Place
Brooklyn, NY 11217
718-622-6659

Freelance scientific, technical, general copy editor, proofreading. Rewriting, developmental editing. Nineteen years experience. Specialties: computers, engineering, electronics, physics, chemistry, mathematics, medicine, anthropology, business, political science, general trade. Computer capability, disk editing. Relocating to Santa Fe, NM.

## Connie Poore

*Los Alamos Historical Society Publications*
PO Box 43
1921 Juniper
Los Alamos, NM 87544
505-662-7374
f: 505-662-6455
rpoore@roadrunner.com
November through March:
505-662-6272
f: 505-662-6312

Human and natural history of Los Alamos, New Mexico area. Development of atomic bomb, including a video with interviews of descendants of area homesteaders, residents, soldiers and scientists from afar. Guidebooks for Bandelier National Monument and Jemez mountains.

## Mary Powell

*Ancient City Press*
PO Box 5401
Santa Fe, New Mexico 87502
505-982-8195
f: 505-982-8195

*Ancient City Press* has been publishing fine regional books on the
Southwest since 1961. We specialize in non-fiction including
folk art, travel, folklore, rock art,
archaeology, folk religion, children's, Native American and
Hispanic titles.

## David M. Prentice

*Vaughan Printing*
411 Cowan St
Nashville, TN 37207
615-256-2244
f: 615-259-4576

*Vaughan Printing* offers state-of-
the-art electronic prepress with
both sheet-fed and web capabilities
with printing from one to four colors. We also offer in house binding
and specialize in short to medium
runs from 500-10,000.

## Ann Racuya-Robbins

*Images For Media*
PO Box 8505
Santa Fe, NM 87504
505-753-3648
f: 505-753-7049
e-mail: arr.ifm.com

*Images For Media* is a multi-media
publishing enterprise dedicated to
contemporary ideas and art. IFM
publishes the literary/art journal
*yefief*, and other books of poetry,
fiction and exploratory forms. Ann
is vice-president of NMBA and
New Mexico Center for the Book.

## Jeff Radford

*Rhombus Publishing Co., Inc.*
PO Box 806
Corrales, NM 87048
505-897-3700

General trade books and
Western Americana.

## Agnesa Reeve

30 Old Arroyo Chamiso
Santa Fe, NM 87505
505-988-3713
f: 505-988-3713
e-mail:
    73160.627@compuserve.com

## Ellen Bradbury Reid

*Recursos de Santa Fe*
826 Camino del Monte Rey
Santa Fe, NM 87505
505-982-0807
f: 505-989-8608
e-mail: recursos@aol

## Lisa Reid

*Ferguson-Carol Publishers*
36 Camino Cielo
Santa Fe, NM 87501
505-983-3303
f: 505-983-3303
e-mail:
76463.3510@compuserve.com

Publishes *Raising Little Kids with
Just a Little Money* by Lisa Reid,
and *Purse Strings* newsletter, for
parents who want to spend less
and enjoy their kids more.
Established 1996.

## Melody Rendon

*Wo-Pila Publishing*
PO Box 84002
Phoenix, AZ 85071
800-786-6322

*My Road to the Sundance* by
Manny Twofeathers. True story of
one man's spiritual journey and
rediscovery of his native roots.
Manny bares his soul, his visions,
his strengths and weaknesses.
Powerful book, hard to put down!

## Paul Rhetts

*LPD Press*
2400 Rio Grande Blvd NW
#1213
Albuquerque, NM 87104
505-344-9382
f: 505-345-5129
e-mail: PAULLPD@aol.com

*LPD Press* publishes general
trade, literature and nonfiction
books, and the new *Tradición
Revista*, a journal of contemporary and traditional Spanish
Colonial art and culture.

## Charles Rosenberg

*Rose Printing Company*
2503 Jackson Bluff Road
Tallahassee, FL 32304
800-227-3725
f: 904-576-4153
e:mail: rose@freenet.fsu.edu

*Rose Printing Company* is a
short-run (250-5,000 copies)
book manufacturer with sheet-fed
and web presses, 1 to 5 colors.
Rose's in-house bindery offers
perfect bound, case-bound, saddle
stitch and lay-flat binding.
Speciality: mini-books.

## Robert E. Ryan

*Braun-Brumfield Inc.*
100 North Stuebler Rd
Ann Arbor, MI 48103
313-662-3241
f: 313-662-1667

Short to medium run complete
book manufacturing; in-house
composition disk-to-film capability, typesetting from disk or manuscript; sheet-fed offset printing;
sewn or adhesive hardcover binding; sewn notch and perfect softcover binding; mailing service.

## Claude M. Saks

*Heartsfire Books*
500 N. Guadalupe St, #G-465
Santa Fe, NM 87501
505-988-5160
f: 505-986-1781

Spirituality and New Age book
publisher.

## M. H. Salmon

*High-Lonesome Books*
26 High-Lonesome Rd
Silver City, NM 88061
505-388-3763

*High-Lonesome Books* publishes
new and reprint volumes of
Southwest Americana and the
outdoors (natural history, hunting, fishing, etc.). We also deal in
used and rare books on the same
subjects.

## Bernadette Sanchez

*Webworks*
1807 Second St, #65
Santa Fe, NM 87505
505-982-3526
e-mail:
webworks@roadrunner.com

*Webworks* designs home pages
for the internet.

## Evalyn Schoppet

*Sterling Publishing Services*
12404 Chelwood Trail NE
Albuquerque, NM 87112
505-271-2866
f: 505-271-2882

Offers full production services
for non-fiction books: project
management, editing, design,
desktop publishing or typesetting,
illustration, indexing, cover
design, printing. Twenty years in
publishing

## Ron Schultz

*Learning Arts*
300 E. Marcy St
Santa Fe, NM 87501
505-466-4577

## Linda Seaman

*Patterson Printing Co.*
1550 Territorial Road
Benton Harbor, MI 49022
800-848-8826, 616-925-2177
f: 616-925-6057

*Patterson Printing Company* is a
full service book printer. We specialize in high quality short and
long runs. Our binding services
include perfect bound, comb,
wire-o and casebinding. We take
time to help publishers new to
the printing process.

## Jeanne Shannon

*The Wildflower Press*
PO Box 4757
Albuquerque, NM 87196
505-296-0691

Small press specializing in poetry, metaphysical subjects, and
alternative healing methods.

## Harish C. Sharma

11412 Brussels Ave NE
Albuquerque, NM 87111
505-298-2881

Engineer and author of short
stories and essays. Fiction deals
with cultural and social interac-
tion of people from India in
United States. Authored two
books: *Profiles in Hope* (short
story collection) and *Environmental Pollution Compliance* (technical book).

## Connie Shelton

*Intrigue Press*
PO Box 456
Angel Fire, NM 87710
505-377-3474
f: 505-377-3526
mystery302@aol.com

Publisher of mystery, suspense
and adventure book-length
fiction. We publish 2-3 titles per
year. List is full until 1998. 1995
lead title: *Deadly Gamble* by
Connie Shelton. 1996: Alex
Matthew's Cassidy McCabe
series.

## Jody Shepard

106 Monte Rey
Los Alamos, NM 87544
505-672-9868

## James Clois Smith Jr.

*Sunstone Press*
PO Box 2321
Santa Fe, NM 87504-2321
505-988-4418
f: 505-988-1025

Publisher of Southwestern US
regional books and notecards
since 1971; also provides book
production services and graphics
services.

## Sarah Smith

*Fulcrum Publishing*
350 Indiana Street, Suite 350
Golden, CO 80401
303-277-1623
f: 303-279-7111

*Fulcrum* publishes for the general trade in the subject areas of travel, gardening, Native American, children's books, outdoors, nature, history, and the West. The company also publishes a line of calendars on similar subjects.

## Cirrelda Snider-Bryan

*La Alameda Press*
9636 Guadalupe Trail NW
Albuquerque, NM 87114
505-897-0285
f: same with warning

Throughout New Mexico, writers of all sorts abound; *La Alameda Press* seeks to cultivate those of local imagination and promote the growth of literary activity in this region. Named after our home turf, we infuse our publishing effort with the spirit of the North Valley - a mixture of funk, elegance, and tenacity. J.B. Bryan is Cirrelda's partner in the business.

## Barbara Somerfield

*Aurora Press Inc.*
PO Box 573
Santa Fe, NM 87504
505-989-9804
f: 505-982-8321

*Aurora Press* is devoted to pioneering books that catalyze personal growth, balance and transformation. It aims to make available, in a digestible format, an innovative synthesis of ancient wisdom and twentieth century resources, integrating esoteric knowledge and daily life. *Aurora* titles specialize in astrology, health, metaphysical philosophies, and the emerging global consciousness.

## Kathleen Sparkes

*White Hart Designs*
1803$^1$/$_2$ Alvarado NE
Albuquerque, NM 87110
505-268-3534

Over ten years experience in art and design, layout and printing. From concept to finished product, design, illustrations, layout, prepress and production, let me help you make a beautiful book!

## Kay Stevens

*Thompson-Shore Inc.*
7300 W. Joy Road
Dexter, MI 48130
313-426-3939
f: 800-706-4545
e-mail: http://www.tshore.com

*Thompson-Shore* is a major short and medium run trade book printer, with many in-house capabilities. State-of-the-art electronic prepress technology.

## Mary Sundstrom

*Mary Sundstrom Illustrations*
1909 Kriss Place, NE
Albuquerque, NM 87112
505-294-0582

Tall, well mannered lover of books seeking projects requiring a classically rendered style. I do full color, black and white and ink drawings for both children and adult literature.

## Michael G. Sutin, Esq.

*Sutin Thayer & Browne*
Fire Stone Plaza
100 North Guadalupe,
  Suite 202
PO Box 2187
Santa Fe, New Mexico 87502
505-988-5521

Poet. Counsel to NMBA, Center for the Book, PEN New Mexico. Member, Live Poet's Society. Chair, PNM's Freedom to Write Committee. Publishes lots of poems about Northern New Mexico weirdness.

## Janet L. Sweitzer

PO Box 2908
Silver City, NM 88062
505-538-5944

Budding author.

## Janina Szpotko-Greene

*Healing Center*
3491 Trinity Dr, Suite C
Los Alamos, NM 87544
505-662-4470

Native of Poland, naturalized U.S. citizen, educated in Europe, Canada, USA. Holds B.S. degree in Physical Therapy. Currently in private practice as healing arts practitioner in Los Alamos. Published author of *The Narrow Path*, by Exceptional Books, Ltd.

## Marylee Thomson

*Santa Fe Institute*
  *& Research Plus*
704 Columbia Street
Santa Fe NM 87505
505/988-3616, 983-0737
f: 505/983-0751
e-mail: mat@santafe.edu

Copy editor, writer for the Santa Fe Institute, a scientific think tank

involved with the study of complexity. I freelance for *Complexity Journal*. Research Plus is my own editing and writing service.

## Charles Townley

*New Mexico State University*
Box 30006, Dept. 3475
Las Cruces, NM 88003
505-646-1508
f: 505-646-6940
ctownley@lib.nmsu.edu

## Peggy Van Hulsteyn

1833 Arroyo Chamiso
Santa Fe, NM 87505
505-982-2337
f: 505-983-0811
e-mail: peggylane@aol.com

Author of *The Birder's Bed and Breakfast* and *Mind Your Own Business: What Every Woman Needs to Know to Get Ahead*.

## Gary Whitlock

*Pueblo Productions*
223 N. Guadalupe
Santa Fe, NM 87501
505-982-7895
f: 505-982-0908
e-mail:
  dzinmuz@unix.net.com

Children's educational and music product development company.

## Skip Whitson

*Sun Publishing Co.*
PO Box 5588
Santa Fe, NM 87502
505-471-5177
f: 505-473-4458

We specialize in reprinting metaphysical classics.

### Jeanie C. Williams

*52 Stone Press*
512 Acequia Madre
Santa Fe, NM 87501
505-988-3092
e-mail: cwabit@aol.com

Jeanie Williams is managing editor of *New Mexico Book View*, serves NMBA as secretary, and has active roles in several literary organizations. *52 Stone Press* promotes poetry, women's issues and fiction.

### Robin Williams

Rt 9 Box 16TH
Santa Fe, NM 87505
505-438-8668

Author of several bestselling computer books.

### Harry Willson

*Amador Publishers*
607 Isleta Blvd SW
PO Box 12335
Albuquerque, NM 87195
800-730-4395, 505-877-4395
f: 505-877-4395
e-mail: amador@indirect.com
web site: http://www.indirect.
  com/www/amador

*Amador Publishers* offers full-length trade paperback books, specializing in fiction and biography of unusual worth and appeal, outside the purview of "mainstream" publishing. We also have several 24-page novelty gift books featuring Southwest themes.

### Elizabeth Wolf

1013 Camino de Chelly
Santa Fe, NM 87505
505-438-3430
f: 505-471-5916

Editor with strong credentials in the book publishing industry.

### Kenna S. Wood

*Mosby Publishing Co.*
7250 Parkway Drive
Hanover, MD 21706
410-712-6871
f: 410-712-4424
e-mail:
  kenna.wood@mosby.com

Until 1996, Kenna had been a partner in Gannon Distributing, the New Mexico book wholesaler specializing in regional titles. Gannon (see listing) recently came under new ownership.

# Book Publishers in New Mexico

The Land of Enchantment has a long and enthusiastic publishing history, with such memorable independent and "mom and pop" endeavors as Spud Johnson's Laughing Horse Press in Taos, Jene and Jetta Lyon's Lightning Tree Press in Santa Fe, Jack D. Rittenhouse's Stagecoach Press, and Walter Goodwin's Rydall Press, which published many of the state's literary classics from the 1930s through the 1950s. In the past decade, the number and variety of presses here has exploded, particularly in the Santa Fe area. Although the smaller presses predominate, heavy hitters such as Bear & Company and John Muir Publications are also part of the New Mexico book publishing success story. (⋟ indicates publishers with NMBA members in management or on staff.)

## AMADOR PUBLISHERS
## P. O. Box 12335
## Albuquerque, NM 87195

**AMADOR PUBLISHERS** specializes in fiction and biography of unusual worth and appeal, outside the purview of "mainstream" publishing. A total of twenty titles presents a wide variety of interests: history, environmental sensitivity, equality, psychological candor, satire, healing.

**Prize-winners:** CAESAR OF SANTA FE: A NOVEL FROM HISTORY, by Tim MacCurdy [Best First Novel, Western Writers of America]; HUNGER IN THE FIRST PERSON SINGULAR: STORIES OF DESIRE AND POWER, by Michelle Miller [Best Book by a New Mexico Woman, New Mexico Press Women].

**Best-sellers:** TWELVE GIFTS: RECIPES FROM A SOUTHWEST KITCHEN, by Adela Amador; DUKE CITY TALES: STORIES FROM ALBUQUERQUE, by Harry Willson; EVA'S WAR: A STORY OF SURVIVAL, by Eva Krutein.

**Acclaimed:** ANCESTRAL NOTES: A FAMILY DREAM JOURNAL, by Zelda Leah Gatuskin; CROSSWINDS: A DARKLY COMIC MODERN WESTERN, by Michael Thomas; THE LITTLE BROWN ROADRUNNER: New Mexico's version of 'THE LITTLE RED HEN,' by Leon Wender; CHRISTMAS BLUES: BEHIND THE HOLIDAY MASK, an anthology by sixty-three remarkably candid writers, dealing with holiday depression.

To order: 1-800-730-4395. Ask for a free catalog.
Distributors: Gannon, Ansel Group, Bookpeople, Last Gasp

## ACEQUIA MADRE PRESS

*Kay Matthews*
Box 6, El Valle Route
Chamisal NM 87521
505/689-2200
f: 505/689-2200

*Acequia Madre Press* publishes regional outdoor guidebooks (hiking, backpacking, and cross-country skiing) that include technical, historical, and environmental information.
We also publish books dealing with environmental issues for both children and adults.

## ADOLFO STREET PUBLICATIONS

*Sandra Dixon, Gene Valdes*
PO Box 490
Santa Fe NM 87504
505/986-2010
f: 505/333-4037

## AMADOR PUBLISHERS

*Harry Willson*
PO Box 12335
607 Isleta Blvd SW
Albuquerque NM 87195
505-877-4395
e-mail: amador@indirect.com
web site:
   http://www.indirect.com/
   www/amador

*Amador* specializes in fiction and biography of unusual worth and appeal. We also publish 24-page novelty gift books with Southwestern themes.

## ANCIENT CITY PRESS

*Mary Powell*
PO Box 5401
Santa Fe NM 87502
505-982-8195
f: 505-982-8195

*Ancient City Press* has been publishing fine regional books on the Southwest since 1961. We specialize in non-fiction, including folk art, travel, folklore, rock art, archaeology, folk religion, childrens', Native American, and Hispanic titles.

## ARROYO PRESS

*Linda G. Harris*
PO Box 4333
Las Cruces NM 88003
505-522-2348, 800-795-2692

*Arroyo Press* features Southern New Mexico writers, photographers, and artists in books about the Southwest. Arroyo Press publishes cloth and quality paperback books on architecture, history, biography, travel, and fiction.

## ARROYO PROJECTS STUDIO

*Sally Blakemore*
Fortaleza Coyote
1413 Second St, 2nd floor
Santa Fe, NM 87501
505-988-2331
f: 505-988-2164

*Arroyo Projects Studio* packages unusual novelty books and products for national and international publishers and other markets. We provide complete design, paper engineering, and print production services.

## ARTISTS & WRITERS PRESS
*Tina Le Marque*
369 Montezuma Street,
    Suite #105
Santa Fe NM 87501

## ASPECTOS CULTURALES
*Roberto Mondragon*
1219 Luisa St.
Santa Fe NM 87501
505-986-0799

## ❧ AURORA PRESS INC.
*Barbara Somerfield*
PO Box 573
Santa Fe NM 87504
505-989-9804
f: 505-982-8321

   *Aurora Press* is devoted to pioneering books that catalyze personal growth, balance and transformation. It aims to make available an innovative synthesis of ancient wisdom and twentieth century resources, integrating esoteric knowledge and daily life. Aurora titles specialize in astrology, health, metaphysical philosophies, and the emerging global consciousness.

**Arroyo Projects Studio**
Fortaleza Coyote
1413 Second Street
Santa Fe, NM 87501
Tel: 505-988-2331
Fax: 505-988-2164

## ❧ A+ PRODUCTIONS
*Janeal Arison, Nancy Avedisian*
PO Box 2444
Santa Fe NM 87504
505-988-4434
f: 505-989-1030

   A+ *Productions* is dedicated to the publication of Suki Stories, a series of career and role modeling books for all girls. The books encourage girls to use their imaginations, explore possibilities, and believe in themselves.

## BARRANCA INC.
Los Alamos NM 87544
505-662-5674

## CLARENCE BASS' RIPPED ENTERPRISES
*Clarence & Carol Bass*
528 Chama NE
Albuquerque, NM 87108
505-266-5858, 266-9123

## BEAR & COMPANY
*Adrian Liberman*
506 Agua Fria St
Santa Fe, NM 87501
505-983-5958, 988-5090

## BENNETT BOOKS
*James Tomarelli*
PO Box 1553
Santa Fe, NM 87504
505-986-1428

## ❧ CAPITAN PUBLISHING COMPANY

*Michael W. McCowen*
PO Box 156
Dexter, NM 88230
505-354-4241

Capitan Publishing Company features New Mexico and Southwestern historical fiction with stories infused with personal insights and self-expressive interpretations.

## ❧ CLEAR LIGHT PUBLISHERS

*Harmon Houghton*
*Marcia Keegan*
823 Don Diego Ave
Santa Fe NM 87501
505-989-9590, 800-253-2747
f:505-989-9519

Clear Light Publishers emphasizes quality trade books about New Mexico and Southwestern culture, art, and photography, plus cookbooks and Tibetan subjects.

## DANRUS PUBLISHERS

*Albert Scharf*
320 Sandoval Street
Santa Fe NM 87501
505-474-5858

## DESERT DREAMS PUBLISHING

PO Box 20382
Albuquerque NM 87154
505-821-3810

## ❧ DONOHO BOOKS

*George Donoho Bayless*
PO Box 804
El Rito, NM 87530
505-581-4574
f: 505-753-7700

## DOVE PUBLICATIONS

*James Scully, editor*
Pecos Benedictine Monastery
Pecos, NM 87552
505-757-6597

## ELESIAN HILLS PUBLISHING CO.

*Ed Dziczek*
PO Box 40693
Albuquerque NM 87196

## ❧ EXCEPTIONAL BOOKS

*Elizabeth Allred*
798 47th Street
Los Alamos NM 87544
505-662-6601
f: 505-662-6601
e-mail:
    70076.730@compuserve.com

History, legends, psychology. We are an eclectic small publisher.

## ❧ FERGUSON-CAROL PUBLISHERS

*Lisa Reid*
36 Camino Cielo
Santa Fe, NM 87501
505-983-3302
f: 505-983-3302
e-mail: 76463.3510@
    compuserve.com

Publishes *Raising Kids With Just a Little Money* and *Pursestrings* newsletter for parents who want to spend less and enjoy their kids more.

---

**Exceptional Books, Ltd.**
798 47th Street
Los Alamos, NM 87544
505-662-6601

Fax 505-662-6601

---

## ৯ 52 STONE PRESS

Jeanie C. Williams
512 Acequia Madre
Santa Fe, NM 87501
505-988-3092
e-mail: cwabit@aol.com

52 Stone Press (a division of
Nora Swan Press) specializes in
poetry, women's issues, general
issues and creative fiction.

## ৯ FLEETWOOD PRESS

Kingsley Hammett
2405 Maclovia Lane
Santa Fe, NM 87505
505-471-4549
f: 505-471-4549

Fleetwood Press features a series
of books on New Mexico furniture which include plans and
drawings to enable woodworkers
to authentically reproduce historic styles from over 400 years of
craft history. First titles are:
Classic New Mexican Furniture
and Spanish Colonial Revival
Furniture of the WPA Period.

## ৯ GOLDEN HEART PUBLICATIONS

Michael Hall
PO Box 6759
Santa Fe NM 87502
505-466-0877

Michael Hall's books, flight
lessons, and Pioneer Journal have
enjoyed worldwide recognition.
Hall's third book, A Beginner's
Guide to True Freedom, is due
this year.

## ৯ HARTMAN PUBLISHING INC.

Mark T. Hartman, publisher
PO Box 91628
Albuquerque NM 87199
505-291-1274
f: 505-291-1284

Educational materials for the
health care industries.

## HEALTH PRESS

Kathleen Schwartz
Thomas Hastings
PO Box 1388
Santa Fe NM 87504
505-982-9373, 800-643-2665
f: 505-983-1733

## ৯ HEARTSFIRE BOOKS

Claude M. Saks,
Oliver Beaudette
500 N. Guadalupe St., G-465
Santa Fe NM 87501
505-988-5160
f: 986-1781
e-mail: spiritroad@aol.com

Spirituality, New Age titles.

## ৯ HIGH-LONESOME BOOKS

Dutch Salmon
26 High-Lonesome Road
Silver City NM 88061
505-388-3763

High-Lonesome Books publishes
new and reprint volumes of
Southwestern Americana and the
outdoors (natural history, hunting,
fishing, etc.). We also deal in used
and rare books on these subjects.

## HIGH MESA PRESS

53 Night Hawk Trail
Las Colonias
Taos NM 87571

## HIGH MOUNTAIN PRESS (OnWord Press, OnLine Press)

*Barbara Kohl, Janet Leigh Dick*
2530 Camino Entrada
Santa Fe NM 87505
505-471-2600, 800-223-6397
f: 505-438-9633

## ◊ IMAGES FOR MEDIA

*Ann Racuya-Robbins*
PO Box 8505
Santa Fe NM 87504
505-753-3648
f: 505-753-7049
e-mail: arr@ifm.com

Images For Media is a multimedia publishing enterprise dedicated to contemporary ideas and art. IFM publishes the literary/art journal *yefief*, and other books of poetry, fiction and exploratory forms.

## ◊ INTRIGUE PRESS

*Connie Shelton*
PO Box 456
Angel Fire NM 87710
505-377-3474
f: 505-377-3526
e-mail: mystery302@aol.com

Publisher of mystery, suspense and adventure book-length fiction. We publish two to three titles per year (list full until

**IMAGES FOR MEDIA**

*A pioneer in the art of publishing*

**505 753-3648**
arr@ifm.com

1998). *Deadly Gamble* by Connie Shelton (1995); Alex Matthew's *Cassidy McCabe* series (1996).

## ◊ JOHN MUIR PUBLICATIONS

*Steven Cary*
PO Box 613
Santa Fe NM 87504
505-982-4078
f: 988-1680

John Muir has been publishing books in Santa Fe since 1969. Currently releases over 60 books per year, with main focus on travel and juvenile non-fiction. JMP engages many independent editors and graphic artists.

## JUNIPER LEARNING

*Jean Yoder*
Route 1, Box 437
PO Drawer D
Española NM 87532

## ◊ KIVA PUBLISHING INC.

*Maurice R. McDonald*
102 E Water St
Santa Fe, NM 87501
(505) 820-7413

## ◊ LA ALAMEDA PRESS

*Cirrelda Snyder-Bryan, J.B. Bryan*
9636 Guadalupe Trail NW
Albuquerque NM 87114
505-897-0285
f: 505-897-0285

Throughout New Mexico, writers of all sorts abound. *La Alameda Press* seeks to cultivate those of local imagination and promote the growth of literary activity in this region. A mixture of funk, elegance and tenacity.

## ⁊ LEARNING ARTS

*Ron Schultz*
300 E. Marcy St
Santa Fe NM 87501
505-466-4577

## LIGHT INSTITUTE PRESS

*Chris Griscom*
HC-75, Box 50
Galisteo, NM 87540
505-466-1975

## ⁊ LPD PRESS

*Paul Rhetts, Barbara Awalt*
2400 Rio Grande Blvd NW,
    #1213
Albuquerque NM 87104
505-344-9382
f: 505-345-5129
e-mail: PAULLPD@aol.com

General trade, literature, nonfiction books. Publishes *Tradición Revista*, a journal of contemporary and traditional Spanish Colonial art and culture.

## LOS ALAMOS BOOKS

PO Box 1432
Los Alamos NM 87544
505-662-6837

## ⁊ LOS ALAMOS HISTORICAL SOCIETY

*Connie Poore*
PO Box 43
Los Alamos NM 87544
505-662-6272
f: 505-662-6312

Human and natural history of Los Alamos area. Publications about the development of the atomic bomb, including a video with interviews of descendants of area homesteaders, residents, soldiers and scientists from afar. Guidebooks for Bandelier National Monument and the Jemez Mountains.

## LA LLORONA PRESS

*Eduardo Kraul*
PO Box 5699
Santa Fe NM 87502

## ⁊ LUMEN, INC.

*Ronald Christ*
40 Camino Cielo
Santa Fe, NM 87501
505-988-5820
f: 505-988-9236
e-mail: site@rt66.com

*Lumen* publishes books on architecture and design.

## ⁊ MARIPOSA PRINTING & PUBLISHING

*Joe Mowrey*
922 Baca Street
Santa Fe NM 87501
505-988-5582

## ⁊ THE MESSAGE COMPANY

*James Berry*
4 Camino Azul
Santa Fe NM 87505
505-474-0998
f: 505-471-2584

*The Message Company* is a publisher specializing in New Energy, New Science, freedom, and new business paradigms. We produce books, audio and video tapes, and other media.

## MOON BEAR PRESS

*Steve Gallegos*
930 Baca Street
Santa Fe NM 87501

## MUNKLINDE VESTERGAARD

*D. Sorensen*
Route 1, Box 126
Nambe NM 87501
505-455-3165

## ࣷ MUSEUM OF NEW MEXICO PRESS

*Ron Latimer*
PO Box 2087
Santa Fe NM 87504
505-827-6454
f: 505-827-7308

MNM *Press* publishes general trade and art quality titles on the arts and cultures of the Southwest and beyond. Subjects include the fine and folk arts, Native American and Hispanic life, anthropology, history, and nature.

## NEW ATLANTEAN PRESS

PO Box 9638
Santa Fe NM 87502
505-983-1856

## ࣷ NEW MEXICO STATE UNIVERSITY LIBRARY PRESS

*Charles Townley*
Box 30006 Dept. 3475
Las Cruces NM 88003
505-646-1508
f: 505-646-6940

## ࣷ OCEAN TREE BOOKS

*Richard Polese*
PO Box 1295
Santa Fe NM 87504
505-983-1412
f: 505-983-1412
e-mail: oceantre@trail.com

*Ocean Tree Books*, founded in 1983, publishes the *Adventure Roads Travel* guidebooks to localities and routes in the Southwest and South, plus inspirational, peacemaking, and local history titles. *Santa Fe on Foot, From Santa Fe to O'Keefe Country* and *Peace Pilgrim's Wisdom* are three of our most popular trade books.

## ࣷ OTOWI CROSSING PRESS

*Colleen Olinger*
1350 Central Ave
Los Alamos, NM 87544
505-662-9589, 455-2691

*Otowi Crossing Press* is operated by Otowi Station Bookstore, a combination general bookstore (specializing in atomic history, technical, and children's books) and a Science Museum store.

## ❧ PENNYWHISTLE PRESS

*Victor Di Suvero, publisher*
PO Box 734
Tesuque NM 87574
505-982-0066
f: 505-982-8116
e-mail: pnywhistle@aol.com

*Pennywhistle Press* began in 1986 as a way to present the work of notable poets. Known for its *Chapbook Series*, Pennywhistle recently expanded its poetry offerings into anthology market with *Saludos! Poemas de Nuevo México* and *Sextet 1: Six Powerful American Voices*. Publications scheduled include *Marilyn, My Marilyn* (over 125 poems about the legendary Marilyn Monroe) and *The Santa Fe Poems*.

## PRESS OF THE PALACE OF THE GOVERNORS

*Pamela Smith, master printer*
PO Box 2087
Santa Fe NM 87503
505-827-6477

Historic letterpress "living exhibit" producing high quality limited editions; a program of the Museum of New Mexico.

## PRO LIBERTATE PUBLISHING / FEHERVARY

1905 Conejo Drive
Santa Fe NM 87501
505-983-8534

## ❧ PROSPECT BOOKS

*Peter Michaelson*
2912 Calle Derecha
Santa Fe NM 87505
505-438-3732

*Prospect Books* is on the cutting edge of psychology and health with titles that explore the hidden aspects of human nature, exposing the ways we create our own failure and unhappiness.

## RADIANT LIGHT PRESS

*Robbie Ravihar Kahlsa*
1505 Llano Street
Santa Fe NM 87505

## ❧ RED CRANE BOOKS

*Marianne &*
  *Michael O'Shaughnessy*
2008 Rosina Street #B
Santa Fe NM 87505
505-988-7070, 800-922-3392
f: 505-989-7476
e-mail:
  crane1@roadrunner.com

*Red Crane Books* is committed to publishing books that foster an understanding of human diversity. Our interest is in art, cooking, how-to, literature, social history, travel, and other areas that complement our list.

## ❧ RED RABBIT PRESS

*Antonio R. Garces*
PO Box 6545
Santa Fe NM 87502
505-982-1773

*Red Rabbit* publishes interviews of citizens' encounters with ghosts: *Adobe Angels: The Ghost of Santa Fe and Taos*, *Adobe Angels: The Ghost of Albuquerque*, and *Adobe Angels: The Ghost of Las Cruces and Southern New Mexico*.

## ❧ RHOMBUS PUBLISHING CO.

*Jeff Radford*
PO Box 806
Corrales NM 87048
505-897-3700

General trade books and Western Americana.

## ROUTE 66 PUBLISHING

*J. Brent Rieks, publisher*
4002 Silver SE
Albuquerque NM 87108
505-268-4478

## RYDAL PRESS

*Clark Kimball*
PO Box 2247
Santa Fe NM 87504
505-983-1680

## SAN MIGUEL PRESS

PO Box 442
Las Vegas NM 87701

## SAUNDERS PUBLISHING CO.

162 South Dal Paso
Hobbs NM 88240

## SCHOOL OF AMERICAN RESEARCH (SAR) PRESS

*Joan O'Donnell, Peter Palmieri*
School of American Research
PO Box 2188
Santa Fe NM 87504
505-984-0741
f: 505-989-9809

## ❧ SHERMAN ASHER PUBLISHING

*Judith Asher*
PO Box 2853
Santa Fe NM 87504
505-984-2686
f: 820-2744
e-mail:
71277.2057@compuserve.com

*Sherman Asher Publishing* is a small press dedicated to the rhythms of adventure, and has already shifted into the new paradigm. Front line reports are available as poetry, non-fiction and CD-ROMs.

## SOUTHWEST NATURAL AND CULTURAL HERITAGE ASSN. (SNCHA)

*Stephen G. Maurer*
*Joanna Hurley*
6501 Fourth St NW, Suite 1
Albuquerque NM 87107
505-345-9498
f: 505-344-1543

## ❧ STATE HOUSE PRESS

Erik J. Mason
1882 Conejo Drive
Santa Fe NM 87505
505-982-1258

State House Press specializes in Texana and reprints of rare books.

## ❧ SUN PUBLISHING CO.

Skip Whitson,
   Robyn Covelli-Hunt
PO Box 5588
Santa Fe NM 87502
505-471-5177
f: 505-473-4458

Sun Publishing specializes in reprinting metaphysical classics.

## ❧ SUNSTONE PRESS

James Clois Smith Jr.
PO Box 2321
Santa Fe NM 87504
505-988-4418, 800-243-5644
f: 505-988-1025

Publisher of Southwestern U.S. regional books and notecards since 1971; also provides book production services and graphics services.

## TIERRA PUBLICATIONS

Carl & Joan Stromquist
4350 Airport Road, #5-612
Santa Fe NM 87505
505-983-6300
f: 505-986-8372

## ❧ TRAILS WEST PUBLISHING

Joe Hayes
PO Box 8619
Santa Fe NM 87504
505-982-8058, 915-566-9072

Trails West was formed by story-teller Joe Hayes to publish audio cassettes to accompany his books. Distributed by Cinco Puntos Press in El Paso, Texas.

## TUTORIAL PRESS

711 Encino Place NE
Albuquerque NM 87102
505-764-0069

## TWIN PALMS PUBLISHERS

401 Paseo de Peralta
Santa Fe, NM 86501
505-988-5717
f: 505-988-7011

Photography.

## ❧ TWO EAGLES PRESS

Paul E. Huntsberger
PO Box 208
Las Cruces NM 88001
505-523-7911

publishers of books dealing with international and intercultural themes (formerly EDITTS… Publishing).

## UNICORN PUBLISHING INC.

3507 Wyoming Blvd NE
Albuquerque NM 87111
505-299-4401

## UNIVERSITY OF NEW MEXICO PRESS

*Peter Moulson*
1720 Lomas Blvd NE
Albuquerque NM 87131
505-277-2346

## VITROGRAPHICS PUBLICATIONS

Santa Fe NM 87504
505-473-9203

## ᏧᏯ WEST END PRESS

*John F. Crawford*
PO Box 27334
Albuquerque NM 87125
505-345-5729
f: 505-345-5729

Southwestern small press publisher in business for 20 years
(ten years in Albuquerque).
West End features Native
American, Spanish/Chicano,
multicultural, women, political
writing, poetry, fiction, drama
(82 titles published, 24 active).

## ᏧᏯ WESTERN EDGE PRESS

*James B. Mafchir*
126 Candelario St
Santa Fe NM 87501
505-988-7214
f: 505-988-7214

Southwestern subjects, book
project management.

## ᏧᏯ THE WILDFLOWER PRESS

*Jeanne Shannon*
PO Box 4757
Albuquerque NM 87196
505-296-0691

*The Wildflower Press* is a small
press specializing in poetry, meta-

physical subjects, and alternative
healing methods.

## WRITING DESIGNS

*Gene Oak*
611 Acoma, Box 5060
Taos NM 87571
505-758-0355
f: 505-758-5647

## ᏧᏯ YUCCA TREE PRESS

*Janie Matson*
2130 Hixon Drive
Las Cruces NM 88005
505-524-2357

*Yucca Tree Press* specializes in
Southwestern and military history.
A new series, *Frontier People and
Forts*, was inaugurated in 1995
with the publication of *Only the
Echoes: The Life of Howard Bass
Cushing*. A new book in the series
will appear every 12-18 months,
available in both paper and a
numbered and signed limited edition.

## ᏧᏯ ZUNI A:SHAWI PUBLISHING

*Wells Mahkee, Jr., coordinator*
*Anne Beckett, manager*
PO Box 3007
Zuni NM 87327
505-782-4880
f: 505-782-2136

*Zuni A:shiwi Publishing* produces
quality books about the distinctive culture of Zuni—and by
focusing on Zuni authors, from
the unique Zuni perspective.
Zuni A:shiwi presents fiction and
non-fiction books for all ages.

# Book Related Organizations

You may find this list of book-related groups in the state one of the most valuable in *New Mexico's Book World*. Through these organizations, you should be able to get in touch with hundreds of people who may not be listed individually (for example: writers, poets, people in funding agencies). Included are brief descriptions of what each organization provides and who they serve. We've listed the New Mexico Book Association first and the rest in alphabetical order.

## New Mexico Book Association (NMBA)

*Richard Polese, president*
PO Box 1295
Santa Fe, NM 87504
505-983-1412
f: 505-983-1412
e-mail: nmba@roadrunner.com
web site:
   www.roadrummer.com/~
   webworks/nmba

  NMBA serves all book people in New Mexico and supports the Book in its many forms. Members are individuals who are professionally involved with books in New Mexico, including publishers, writers, editors, indexers, designers, production and service bureau people, librarians, booksellers, distributors, printers, and readers. Monthly lunch or dinner meetings. Publishes monthly *Libro* newsletter and *New Mexico's Book World, A Resource Guide*. NMBA was founded in 1994.

## Border Book Festival

*Denise Chavez, Susan L. Tweit,*
  *co-directors*
224 N. Campo St
Las Cruces, NM 88001
505-524-1499

  Annual book event in the El Paso/Las Cruces area.

## Live Poets Society

*Richard Brandt*
433 Paseo de Peralta, #101
Santa Fe, NM 87501
505-989-3322, 989-9300

  Annual public reading in June, bimonthly members meeting.

## Mountain & Plains Booksellers Association

*Lisa Knudsen, executive director*
805 LaPorte Ave
Fort Collins, CO 80521
970-484-5856
800-752-0249
f: 970-407-1479

  Regional association of book retailers and wholesalers. Annual Fall Trade Show. Publishes MPBA newsletter and *A Guide to the Mountains and Plains Bookselling Market.*

## New Mexico Arts Division

*Lara Morrow, director*
*Judyth Hill, literary coordinator*
Office of Cultural Affairs
La Villa Rivera Building
228 E. Palace Ave
Santa Fe, NM 87501
505-827-6490
800-879-4278

  Publishes *The Handy Dandy Guide to Grants, Awards and Resources for New Mexico Writers* (free); Tumblewords grant programs; brochure of writers; advocates National Poetry Month in New Mexico. Judyth Hill's home address: HL 69, Box 20H, Sapello, NM 87745, 505-454-9628.

## New Mexico Book League

*Carol Myers, editor*
8632 Horacio Place NE
Albuquerque, NM 87111
505-299-8940
f: 505-284-8032

Publishes the highly respected *New Mexico Book Talk*, which reviews any and all books published in or written about New Mexico. Founded in 1971, NMBL is a catalyst for everyone involved in Southwestern literature. Approximately 500 subscribers in 44 states.

## New Mexico Center for the Book

*Marsie Cate, president*
3922 Old Santa Fe Trail
Santa Fe, NM 87505
505-983-1516
f: 505-983-1391

Formed in 1996 in cooperation with the Library of Congress, the New Mexico State Library, Albuquerque Public Library, WESTAF, and the New Mexico Book Association. Supports reading, writing, literacy, and publishing programs in New Mexico; quarterly newsletter. (NMBA members were instrumental in the Center's creation.) See also entry for New Mexico State Library.

## New Mexico Coalition for Literacy

*Michelle Jaschke,*
*executive director*
1510 St. Francis Drive
PO Box 6085
Santa Fe, NM 87502
505-982-3997
800-233-7587
f: 505-982-4095

Training and technical assistance services for literary programs throughout New Mexico.

## New Mexico Library Association

*Kathy Flanary, president*
11200 Montgomery Blvd SE
Albuquerque, NM 87111
505-292-9883
f: 505-322-2425
*Virginia Seiser, contact*
1224 Monroe NE
Albuquerque, NM 87110

Statewide organization of public, school, and institutional librarians. Annual conference. Kathy Flanary's address is: New Mexico School for the Visually Handicapped, 1900 White Sands Blvd., Alamogordo, NM 88310; 505-437-3505, ext. 129.

## New Mexico Library Foundation

*Karen Watkins, secretary*
P.O. Box 30527a
Albuquerque, NM 87190
800-876-2203

## New Mexico Literary Arts

*Ron Chalmers*
512 Acequia Madre
Santa Fe, NM 87501
505-988-3092
e-mail: cwabit@aol.com

Created in 1996 by members of the former Poetry Center of New Mexico and others involved in the literary arts.

## New Mexico State Library

*Karen Watkins, state librarian*
325 Don Gaspar Ave
Santa Fe, NM 87501
505-827-3800, 800-759-7687
f: 505-827-3888
e-mail:
  kwatkins@stlib.state.nm.us

State agency. Will be moving in 1997 to new location on Cerrillos Road to be shared with New Mexico State Records Center and Archives.

## PEN New Mexico

*Richard Harris, president*
*Dorothy Doyle, secretary*
2860 Plaza Verde
Santa Fe, NM 87505
505-473-4813

An organization of literary professionals dedicated to the freedom of expression. A chapter of PEN Center USA West. *Pen on Paper* (bimonthly newsletter). Established in 1992.

## Recursos de Santa Fe

*Ellen Bradbury Reid,*
  *executive director*
825 Camino del Monte Rey
Santa Fe, NM 87505
505-984-3077, 982-0807
f: 505-989-8608
e-mail: recursos@aol

Nonprofit arts and literary organization. Sponsored Libros Book Fair in Santa Fe in 1995 and the Wholesale Gift Show in 1996.

## Rocky Mountain Book Publishers Association

*Alan Bernhard,*
  *executive director*
P.O. Box 19013
Boulder, CO 80308
303-447-2320
f: 303-447-9710

Founded in New Mexico in 1977, RMBPA is a trade and professional organization of publishers throughout 13 Western states. Annual Conference (usually held in Colorado or New Mexico). Publishes *The End Sheet* (quarterly newsletter), and annual *RMBPA Catalog & Directory*. Margaret Griffin is RMBPA's New Mexico representative, 505-820-7526.

## Society of the Muse of the Southwest

*Phyllis Hotch*
P.O. Box 3225
Taos, NM 87571
505-758-0081, 438-3249(h)

Taos writers organization dedicated to supporting the practice and appreciation of the literary arts in northern New Mexico. Presents readings, workshops, conferences and community projects.

### Southwest Literary Center

*William J. Higginson*
PO Box 2740
Santa Fe, NM 87504
505-988-5, 22, 438-3249
f: 505-989-8608

Originated with Recursos. Sponsors six national writers conferences and 40 public readings a year.

### Western States Arts Federation (WESTAF)

*Anthony Radich,*
*executive director*
1543 Champa St, #220
Denver, CO 80202
303-629-1166
f: 303-629-9717

Offers programming, funding and technical assistance to arts and literary people and organizations in 12 states. Western States Book Awards program helps regional publishers (contact Robert Sheldon, 206-706-8066). (WESTAF completed a move from Santa Fe to Denver in October 1996.)

### World Poetry Bout Association

*Anne McNaughton*
52755NDCBU
Taos, NM 87571
505-758-1800

Sponsors Taos Poetry Circus, including World Championship Poetry Bout in Taos in June.

### The Writers Group

*Elaine Coleman, contact*
899 Zia Road
Santa Fe, NM 87505
505-983-9747
e-mail: elaine@trail.com

Salon of Santa Fe women writers who explore writing issues.

# Booksellers In New Mexico

New Mexico's booksellers are organized here in six sections: **Independent Bookstores**, **Antiquarians**, **Christian Bookstores**, **National Chain** stores, **Mail Order** services, and **Institutions** (college and museum) stores. Wherever possible, the name of the owner and/or manager and bookbuyer are also listed. We've tried to include the specialties of the independent stores and antiquarians. Christian bookstores range from Baptist to Catholic to Mormon, and several serve a broad religious market. National chains, usually located in shopping centers, sometimes include (or are dominated by) large video sections.

There's an ominous trend in bookselling today. Many independent stores, filled with character and owned by true bibliophiles, have been dropping by the wayside as huge national conglomerates move into the malls. The marketing budgets and discounting policies of big publishers and distributors have put the squeeze on many smaller, more innovative publishers and bookstores. Managers of some chain outlets are unfamiliar with books of local or regional interest. Yet here in New Mexico, despite the loss of such legendary stores as Cantwell's in Albuquerque and Los Artesanos in Las Vegas, new and dedicated entrepreneurs continue to take the plunge into bookselling. NMBA supports retail bookselling in New Mexico in all its forms.

## INDEPENDENT BOOKSTORES

### ABC Book & Gift Shop
*Sharon Oldham, owner*
146 N. Third
PO Box 115
Raton, NM 87740
505-445-8454
f: 505-445-3373

Cooking, religion, Southwest, children's.

### Ace Trading Co., Inc.
*Bob Brooks, president*
*Ernest M. Garcia, manager*
111 N. Main St
Clovis, NM 88101-7550
505-762-4848

Adventure, mystery, detective, romance, science fiction, fantasy.

### Alla
*James J. Dunlap and*
*Barbara A. Sommer, owners*
102 W. San Francisco St,
   Suite 20
Santa Fe, NM 87501
505-988-5416

Spanish language, art, history, anthropology, archaeology of the Americas.

### Anthropology Film Center Bookstore
*Carroll Warner Williams,*
  *owner*
1626 Canyon Road
Santa Fe, NM 87501
505-983-4127

Films, filmmaking, French, Spanish.

### The Ark
*Joan Aon, et al, owners*
133 Romero St
Santa Fe, NM 87501
505-988-3709
f: 505-982-0913

New Age, healing, psychology, astrology, channeling, meditation.

### The Aspen Tree
*Jane Deyo, owner*
2340 Sudderth Dr
PO Box 367
Ruidoso, NM 88345
505-257-4088

Fiction, nonfiction, Southwest, hummingbirds.

### Aztec Photo & Books
*Henry A. Jackson, owner*
120 S. Main Ave
Aztec, NM 87410
505-334-6221

Photography, nonfiction, archaeology.

### Barry's Used Books
*Barry J. Digman, owner*
111 N. Allen
Farmington, NM 87401
505-327-5548

Used paperback.

### Best Price Books & Coffee
*Alan Price, owner, manager*
1800 Central SE
Albuquerque, NM 87106
505-842-0624

General, used.

## Birdsong Used Books & Records

Brad & Claudia Bumgarner-
  Kirby, owners, managers
139 Harvard Dr SE
Albuquerque, NM 87106
505-268-7204

Used paperback, science fiction, fantasy, literature.

## The Blue-Eyed Indian Bookshop

Lee Marmon, owner
Kathy Marmon, manager
Laguna Reservation
Interstate 40, Exit 108
Casa Blanca, NM 87007
t/f: 505-552-6264

General, history.

## Blue Moon Books & Vintage Video

Carmen Blue, owner
329 Garfield St
Santa Fe, NM 87501
505-982-3035

Metaphysical, psychology, poetry, women's literature, feminist.

## Boat of Angels

Thelma Cook, Connie Mann,
  owners, managers
1720 S. Telshor, Suite B
Las Cruces, NM 88011
505-521-3161

New Age, metaphysical, occult, psychological, self-development.

## A Book Affair

1496 S. Solano Dr
Las Cruces, NM 88005
505-522-5515

## The Bookcase

Laura Eisner, owner
109 Mesa SE
Albuquerque, NM 87106
505-247-3102

Used class studies, cooking, metaphysics, occult, foreign language.

## Book Fare, Food for Thought

Ms. Bing LeRoy, owner,
  manager
13625 Cedarbrook NE
Albuquerque, NM 87111
505-296-4575

Pets, livestock, farming, ranching.

## The Book Rack

Carol Riner, owner
2506 Juan Tabo Blvd NE
Albuquerque, NM 87112
505-292-0397

Religious, juvenile, bestsellers.

## Books & More Books

Leo Romero, owner
1341 Cerrillos Road
Santa Fe, NM 87501
505-473-5508

Used western, philosophy, religious, art, fiction.

## The Book Store

Kate Winner-Carothers, owner
1031 Mechem Dr
Ruidoso, NM 88345
505-258-3663

General, philosophy, spiritual.

### Bookworks
*Nancy Rutland, owner*
4022 Rio Grande Blvd NW
Albuquerque, NM 87107
505-344-8139
f: 505-344-8139
  (call first for fax)

Art, Southwest, cooking, travel, gardening.

### Bowlin's Mesilla Book Center
*Mary Alice Bowlin, owner*
On the Plaza
PO Box 96
Mesilla, NM 88046
505-526-6220

General, Southwest.

### Bridge Street Books & Coffeehouse, Ltd.
*Peter Du Mont, president*
131 Bridge St
Las Vegas, NM 87701
505-454-8211

History, poetry, Southwest.

### Brodsky Bookshop
*Morris Witten, contact*
218 Paseo del Pueblo Norte
PO Box 1529
Taos, NM 87571
505-758-9468

Southwest, Native Americans.

### Brotherhood of Life
*Richard E. Buhler, president*
*Graham Dodd,*
  *vice-president, manager*
110 Dartmouth SE
Albuquerque, NM 87106
505-873-2179

New Age, astrology, Eastern philosophy, health.

### Caldwell & Campbell Dealers in Books
*Pat & John Caldwell,*
  *owners*
3002 Wilson Pl NE
Albuquerque, NM 87106
t/f: 505-266-6704

Travel; Irish, Scottish, Welsh.

### Charrah's, Another Story
*Charlotte Prossen, owner*
Historic Old Town
328 San Felipe NW
Albuquerque, NM 87104
505-243-9588

New Mexicana, children's, Native American.

### Church of Religious Science of Santa Fe Bookstore
*Anna McParthon, manager*
505 Camino de los Marquez
Santa Fe, NM 87501
505-983-5022

Metaphysics, psychology, religious, women's studies, men's issues.

### Classic News Agency
*Vince Bergman, owner*
129 E. Third
PO Box 487
Roswell, NM 88202
505-622-0121

General.

### COAS, My Bookstore
*Patrick H. Beckett, owner*
317 N. Downtown Mall
Las Cruces, NM 88001
505-524-8471

Anthropology, western, history; new and used.

*Branch:*
## COAS Books
*Mike Beckett, manager*
535 S. Melendres
Las Cruces, NM 88005
505-524-0301

## Cobean Stationery Co. Book Dept.
*Mr. & Mrs. L. A. McPherson, owners*
*Donna Groseclose, manager*
320 N. Richardson
PO Box 1598
Roswell, NM 88202
505-622-1922
f: 505-622-3811

Cooking, gardening, religion, western, art, hobbies.

## Colborn of New Mexico, Inc.
*Mary Sharp, manager*
5017 Lomas Blvd NE
Albuquerque, NM 87110
505-262-2066

Elementary high texts, juvenile.

## Collected Works Bookshop
*Lynne Moor, owner*
208-B W. San Francisco St
Santa Fe, NM 87501
505-988-4226

General, Southwest.

## Conflict Management, Inc.
*Jackie Mascarenas, manager*
3900 Georgia NE
Albuquerque, NM 87110
505-884-9411
f: 505-883-6177

Self-development, parenting, co-dependency, alcoholism.

## The Dana Bookstore
*Gladys Dana, owner*
Val Verde Hotel
203 Manzanares
Socorro, NM 87801
800-524-3434, 505-835-3434

General, Southwest, science fiction, children's books. Open 9am to 9pm every day.

## Desert Dreams
*Cynthia Winn, manager*
106 W. Hill Ave
Gallup, NM 87301-6218
505-863-4616

New Age, metaphysical, personal growth.

## Discovery Bookstore
*Richard Pate, manager*
1540 Juan Tabo NE
Albuquerque, NM 87112
505-293-2959

New Age, self-help, metaphysical.

## Don Fernando's Indian Art
*Ernest Montoya, owner*
104 W. Plaza
Taos, NM 87571
505-758-3791

Southwest.

## Don's Paperback Books
*Margaret M. Pierce, owner*
1013 San Mateo Blvd SE
Albuquerque, NM 87108
505-268-0520

Science fiction, fantasy.

### Earth Vision Catalog
*Jaya Bear, manager*
PO Box 1950
El Prado, NM 87529
505-758-1491

Natural, environmental, Native American studies, spirituality.

### Earthwalk
*Wilda A. Lawler, owner*
401 Romero St
Albuquerque, NM 87104
505-242-3217

Metaphysical, regional, multi-cultural, Spanish language.

### The Enchanted Sunmark
*Terry Tipkin, owner*
2400 N. Main
Clovis, NM 88101
505-762-2044

Southwestern, children's.

### Enchanting Land
*Charmaine & Cliff Coimbra,*
*owners*
DeVargas Center Mall
179-B Paseo de Peralta
Santa Fe, NM 87501
505-988-2718
f: 505-989-7404

Children's, natural, science.

### Eureka! Books!
*Dorothy Best, manager*
115 S. Second St
Raton, NM 87740
t/f: 505-445-8658

Fiction, science fiction, fantasy, travel, Southwest, hispanic.

### The Family Bookshelf
*Mollie Petsonk, owner;*
*Buddy Petsonk, manager*
520 W. Main
Artesia, NM 88210
505-746-9077

Used fiction, horror, mystery, science fiction, fantasy.

### Family Bookstore
*Gary Ross, owner*
Bel Aire Shopping Center
2311 N. Jefferson
Hobbs, NM 88240
505-393-6245

Used paperback.

### Farmington Magazine & Book
*Tom Fawcett, owner*
*Kathy Gurule, manager*
218 W. Main
Farmington, NM 87401
505-325-5562

*Branch:*
### Village Book & Hallmark
*Catherine Fawcett, manager*
Animas Valley Mall
4601 E. Main
Farmington, NM 87402
505-327-1150

### La Fonda Newsstand
*Jo Glicksberg, manager*
La Fonda Hotel
100 E. San Francisco St
Santa Fe, NM 87501
505-988-1404

Native American, geographic history, Southwestern architecture, travel.

## Full Circle Books

Anne Grey Frost,
   Mary A. Morrell, owners
2205 Silver Ave SE
Albuquerque, NM 87106
505-266-0022

Feminist, gay & lesbian, mystery, detective, multicultural, children's.

## Garcia Street Books

Greg Ohlsen, owner
376 Garcia St
Santa Fe, NM 87501
505-986-0151
f: 505-986-0151

General, art, architecture.

## Green Spray Books

James Taylor, owner
2400 N. Grimes, Unit B-18
Hobbs, NM 88240
505-392-6515

Science fiction, fantasy.

## Historical Footsteps USA

Barbara A. Teetzel, president
James R. Teetzel, vice president
Plaza Don Luis, Suite 205
305 Romero NW
Albuquerque, NM 87104
505-243-4656

Southwestern Americana.

*Branch:*

211 Old Santa Fe Trail
Santa Fe, NM 87501
505-982-9297

## High-Lonesome Books

M. H. Dutch, Cherie Salmon,
   owners
PO Box 878
Silver City, NM 88062
505-388-3763

Regional, western Americana, natural history.

## Holman's, Inc.

Anthony T. Trujillo, president
6201 Jefferson NE
Albuquerque, NM 87109
505-343-0007
f: 505-343-3509

Science, technology, medicine.

## Horizons Nature & Science

Rick & Holiday Vaill, owners
328 S. Guadalupe St, No. 6
Santa Fe, NM 87501-2649
505-983-1554

Science, nature, environment.

## Jan's Exchange

Donald L. Walsh, owner
3719 Fourth St NW
Albuquerque, NM 87107
505-345-2182

General, used.

## Leighton's Gifts

Roy Dean, Nancy Leighton,
   owners
Nancy Leighton, manager
10 Main St
Clayton, NM 88415
505-374-2721

Poetry, fiction, biblical, cooking.

## Living Batch LTD Books & Periodicals

*Kevin Paul, manager, buyer*
106 Cornell SE
Albuquerque, NM 87106
505-262-1619

Fiction, philosophy, poetry, psychology.

## Maya Books

*Steve Kalminson, manager*
PO Box 13
Cerrillos, NM 87010
505-473-3641
f: 505-473-3641

General.

## Me & Max's Books 'N Things

*Donna-Rae Marquez, manager*
305 N. Main St
Roswell, NM 88201
505-625-2591

General.

## Menaul Book Exchange

*Rosalie Uffer, owner, manager*
9409 Menaul Blvd NE
Albuquerque, NM 87112
505-299-7503

Used foreign language, juvenile, paperback.

*Branch:*

## Alameda Book Exchange

1111 Alameda Blvd NW
Albuquerque, NM 87114
505-898-1298

Used paperback.

## Moby Dickens Bookshop of Taos

*Arthur & Susan Bachrach,*
  *owners*
*Willi Wood,*
  *Patricia McComb, buyers*
John Dunn House #6
124-A Bent Street
Taos, NM 87571
505-758-3050

Art, Southwest, self-development, fiction, natural, women, religion.

## Moondancer Books & Gifts

*Marie Markesteyn, manager*
520 Riverside Dr
Española, NM 87532
505-753-2457
f: 505-753-9478

Metaphysical, self-help, women's studies, Native American.

## Mountain Light Bookstore, Inc.

*Joan Jordan, owner, manager*
PO Box 271
12478 N Hwy 14
Sandia Park, NM 87047
505-281-6738

General.

## Murder Unlimited

*Natalie J. Mackler, owner*
2510 San Mateo Pl NE
Albuquerque, NM 87110
505-884-5491

Mystery, detective, true crime.

## Newsland

*Roger Walsh, owner*
2112 Central SE
Albuquerque, NM 87106
505-242-0694

Mass-market paperbacks, magazines.

## Oasis Books

*Russell Wiegman, owner*
625 Amherst Dr NE
Albuquerque, NM 87106
505-268-1054

Used history, literature.

## 1001 Remedies

*Pami Singh, owner*
123-A Harvard SE
Albuquerque, NM 87106
505-268-7467
f: 505-266-4273

Health, philosophy, herbal.

## Old Santa Fe Trail Books & Coffeehouse

*Tonia & Alan Gould, owners*
613 Old Santa Fe Trail
Santa Fe, NM 87501
505-988-8878
f: 505-983-1398

General, Southwest, cooking, children's, fiction, nonfiction, travel, parenting, poetry.

## Open Mind Bookstore

*Rick Cramer, owner,manager*
119 Harvard SE
Albuquerque, NM 87106
505-262-0066

Metaphysics, co-dependency, Eastern religion, psychic.

## Page One

*Steve & Yvette Stout, owners*
11018 Montgomery Blvd NE
Albuquerque, NM 87111
800-521-4122

General, computer, music, used.

*Branch:*
## Page One Too!

11018 Montgomery NE
Albuquerque, NM 87111
t: 505-294-2026
f: 505-294-5576

Southwestern, general, computer science, technology, used.

## Palace Avenue Books

*Judy Dwyer, owner, manager*
209 E. Palace Ave
PO Box 8390
Santa Fe, NM 87504
505-986-0536

Philosophy, metaphysics, Southwest, history of ideas.

## Photo-Eye

*Rixon Reed, owner*
376 Garcia Street
Santa Fe, NM 87501
505-988-5152
f: 505-988-4955

Photography, art.

## RBooks

*Les Redman, owner*
1715 Iris
Los Alamos, NM 87544
505-662-7257

Scientific, technical, science fiction.

## Rachel's Books

*Rachel Hess, owner*
532 Washington NE
Albuquerque, NM 87108
505-260-0032

Southwestern literature.

## Railyard Books

*Carol Parker, owner*
*Jean Schaumberg, manager*
*Onida Brooks, assistant manager*
340 Read St
Santa Fe, NM 87501
505-995-0533

General, sheet music.

## Readmore Bookstore

*David & Sary Short, owners*
307 E. Tucumcari Blvd
Tucumcari, NM 88401
505-461-3108

Southwest.

## Read On!

*Forrest Furman, manager*
10131 Coors Blvd NW
Albuquerque, NM 87114
505-898-0000
f: 505-898-0110

General, Southwest.

## Recreational Equipment, Inc.

*Dave Brendsel, manager*
1905 Mountain Road NW
Albuquerque, NM 87104
505-247-1191
f: 505-242-9947

Recreation.

## Rio Grande Sun

*Robert Trapp, owner*
238 N. Railroad
PO Box 790
Española, NM 87532
505-753-2126
f: 505-753-2140

Southwest.

## The Santa Fe Bookseller

*Jan. V. Nelson, owner*
223 N. Guadalupe, #285
Santa Fe, NM 87501
505-983-5278
f: 505-989-7681

Art, Southwest.

## The Serenity Shop

*Ann Holmes, owner*
3401 San Mateo NE
Albuquerque, NM 87110
505-889-0885
f: 505-889-0250

Self-help.

## Shalako Shop

*Mr. & Mrs. Edward B.*
  *Grothus, owners*
Community Center
PO Box 970
Los Alamos, NM 87544
505-662-4493

Southwest, Los Alamos history, atomic bomb.

## She Said

*Candra Bryson, owner*
De Vargas Mall
177-B Paseo de Peralta
Santa Fe, NM 87501
505-986-9196

A woman's bookstore "For all of us."

## Silver Office Supply & Bookstore

Tom Earlywine, owner
Susan J. Schiowitz, buyer
117 E. College Ave
Silver City, NM 88061
505-388-3475
f: 505-388-5040

Western.

## Simmons & Simmons Fine Books & Booksearch

Byrd Simmons, owner
Melanie Simmons, manager
Classic Century Square
    Antiques
4616 Central SE
Albuquerque, NM 87108
505-260-1620

Needlecraft, cooking, history, Southwest, European history.

## Sisters' and Brothers'

Daniel Newman, manager
4011 Silver SE
Albuquerque, NM 87108
505-266-7317

Gay & lesbian studies.

## Stagecoach Books & Gifts

John Hoffsis, owner, manager
2021 Old Town Road NW
Albuquerque, NM 87104
505-842-6799

New Mexicana, children's, Old West, Native American.

## T&T Books West

Toby Lujan, owner
Coronado Shopping Center
520 W. Cordova Road
Santa Fe, NM 87501
505-983-3080

General, Southwest.

## Talico, Inc.

Kathy Scioli, owner
1301 N. Prince
Clovis, NM 88101
505-763-7720

General.

## Tasha's Paperback Book Exchange

Natalie J. Mackler, owner
2510 San Mateo Pl NE
Albuquerque, NM 87110
505-884-5491

Mystery, detective, nonfiction, romance.

## The Taos Bookshop, Inc.

Deborah Sherman, owner
Susanna Tvede, manager
122-D Kit Carson Road
Taos, NM 87571
505-758-3733

Native American, Southwest, local history, children's, fiction, nonfiction.

## The Teapot Dome

Dan Lucus, owner, manager
200 S. Gold Ave
Deming, NM 88030
505-546-2828

New Mexicana, how-to.

## 10 Directions Books

Allan Clevenger, owner
PO Box 330
Taos, NM 87571
505-758-2725

Art, biography, metaphysical, occult, religion, Southwest, American history.

### Torreon Trading Co
*Rosina Locke, owner*
Box 117
Lincoln, NM 88338
505-653-4370

Southwest, Lincoln County War, Billy the Kid.

### Universal Supply Centre
*Dean Berenz, owner, manager*
PO Box 25643
Albuquerque, NM 87125
505-265-6557
f: 505-847-2817

Metaphysics, occult, self-development, psychological.

### Vitality Unlimited Bookstore
*Sylvia Garcia, manager*
513 Camino de los Marquez
Santa Fe, NM 87501
505-983-5557
f: 505-983-7064

Health food, general health.

### Words & Wisdom Bookstore
*Sandra McGill, owner, manager*
9221 Coors NW, Suite 2
Albuquerque, NM 87114
505-899-9697
f: 505-898-2557

Metaphysics, self-help, New Age.

### Yucca News Stand
*Adlea Wallace, owner*
*Brian Patrick, manager*
211 Tenth St
Alamagordo, NM 88310
505-437-5296

## ANTIQUARIAN

### Antiquarian-Southwestern Americana
*Mr. and Mrs. F. J. Schaaf, owners*
2362 Union St
Alamagordo, NM 88310
505-437-6369

American, New Mexicana, Texana.

### The Book Addict
*Richard Wyndham, owner*
PO Box 9134
Albuquerque, NM 87119
505-865-5566

Archaeology, exploration, mountaineering.

### The Book Garden
*Diane Lewis, owner*
1502-A Wyoming NE
Albuquerque, NM 87112
505-292-6005

Southwestern, children's.

### Bookstop Albuquerque
*Gerald Lane & Laurie Allen, owners*
University Area Store
3412 Central SE
Albuquerque, NM 87106
505-268-8898

General.

### Curiouser & Curiouser
*Susan Steinman, owner, manager, buyer*
PO Box 274
Santa Fe, NM 87504
505-988-5840

Juvenile.

## DuMont Maps & Books

*Andre & Carol DuMont*
301 E. Palace Ave, #1
Santa Fe, NM 87501
505-988-1076
f: 505-986-6114

Collectible maps and Western
Americana.

## Great Southwest Books

*Clark Kimball, owner*
PO Box 2247
Santa Fe, NM 87504
505-983-1680

New Mexicana, Rydal Press.

## Bob Fein, Books

*Bob Fein, owner*
2156 Candelero St
Santa Fe, NM 87505
505-471-3886

North & South American,
Western, Eskimo, pre-Colombian,
Mexican muralists.

## Hummingbird Books

*Gail Baker, owner*
2400 Hannett NE
Albuquerque, NM 87106
505-268-6277

Travel, literature, women
writers.

## Robert Loren Link, Bookseller

*Robert L. Link, Charles*
*Renteria, owners*
PO Box 511
Las Cruces, NM 88004
505-527-2254

Poetry, 19th & 20th century literature, first editions.

## T. N. Luther, Books

*T. N. Luther, owner*
PO Box 429
Taos, NM 87571
505-776-8117

Archaeology, ethnic, Native
American, Indian artifacts.

## Margolis & Moss

*David Margolis, Jean Moss,*
*owners*
129 W. San Francisco St
PO Box 2042
Santa Fe, NM 87504
505-982-1028
f: 505-982-3256

Western Americana,
photography.

## Numismatic & Philatelic Arts of Santa Fe

*Art Rubino, owner*
PO Box 9712
Santa Fe, NM 87504
t/f: 505-982-8792

Numismatics, archaeology, phi-
latelics, occult (dowsing).

## Nicholas Potter, Bookseller

*Nicholas Potter, owner*
203 E. Palace Ave
Santa Fe, NM 87501
505-983-5434

Photography, Southwest, modern literature.

## Rachel's Books

*Rachel Hess, owner*
532 Washington NE
Albuquerque, NM 87108
505-260-0032

Southwestern literature.

## Charlotte Rittenhouse

600 Solano Dr SE
Albuquerque, NM 87196
505-255-2479

Western Americana,
Stagecoach Press.

## G. Robinson,
## Old Prints & Maps

*George Robinson, owner*
124-D Bent St
Taos, NM 87571
505-758-2278
f: 505-758-1606

Prints, early miniature maps,
mail order.

## Santa Fe
## House of Books

*S. S. Margolis, CEO*
PO Box 23503
Santa Fe, NM 87502
505-473-5161

Native American, arts & crafts,
ethnic, Southwestern, fiction.

## Territorial Editions, Inc.
## —Rare Books

*Gene B. Kuntz, president*
*Patricia D. Kuntz, secretary &*
   *treasurer*
PO Box 8394
Santa Fe, NM 87504
505-983-8346

History, territorial imprints,
Southwestern writers.

## Tom Davies Bookshop

*Eric Holmes Patterson, owner*
3904-B Central SE
Albuquerque, NM 87102
505-247-2072

Native American, art,
Southwest.

# CHRISTIAN

## Baptist Book Store

*Lee Ann Bell, manager*
4770 Montgomery Blvd NE
   Suite 120
Albuquerque, NM 87102
505-881-3322
f: 505-881-4974

## Baptist Book Store

*Mike Goff, manager*
Glorieta Baptist
   Conference Center
Glorieta, NM 87535
505-757-6484
f: 505-757-6149

## Bibles Plus

*Marc Guggino, owner*
2740 Wyoming NE, #13
Albuquerque, NM 87111
505-275-0330

## Bread of Life
## Christian Country Store

*Nancy & Joseph Martinez &*
   *Bonne Conrad, partners*
116 Morningside SE
Albuquerque, NM 87108
505-265-4995

## Bread of Life
## Christian Supplies

*John V. & Leah M. Grove,*
   *owners*
*Leah M. Grove, manager*
104 S. Boardman
Gallup, NM 87301
505-863-3151
f: 505-863-3938

## The Catholic Store
*Guy McIntyre, manager*
4212 Fourth St NW
Albuquerque, NM 87107
505-344-9946

## The Chapel Bookstore
*Paul Scozzafava, manager*
4001 Osuna Road NE
Albuquerque, NM 87109
505-344-2728

## Christian Books & Gifts
*John Gibson, owner*
*Winky Gibson, manager*
1308 Silver Heights Blvd
Silver City, NM 88061
505-388-2115

## Christian Crossing
*Connie Podruchny, owner*
522 E. Idaho Ave
Las Cruces, NM 88001
505-526-1421

*Branch:*
## The Saltshaker
1490 Missouri
Las Cruces, NM 88001
505-522-2553

## Christian Supply Center
*James & Anita Allen, owners*
5310 Menaul NE
Albuquerque, NM 87110
505-881-4811
505-881-7711

## Cornerstone Books Etc.
*Joe Cieszinski, manager*
1722 Saint Michaels Dr,
   Suite A
Santa Fe, NM 87505
505-473-0306

## Glory Be
*Dave & Jan Hedlund, owners*
*Dave Hedlund, manager*
Mesa shopping Center
1020 N. Butler
Farmington, NM 87401
505-325-8711

## The Good Neighbor Christian Bookstore
*Robert Schrag, manager*
2103 W. Main St
PO Box 1230
Farmington, NM 87499
505-325-1343
f: 505-325-9035

## Harvest Christian Books
*John Thomas, owner*
*Delores Black, manager*
10131 Coors Road NW
Albuquerque, NM 87114
505-898-2577

## Inspirations Unlimited
*Tamara Rhoads, owner*
*Larry Rhoads, manager*
2810-F N. Main
Roswell, NM 88201
505-622-5115

## Joshua's Christian Store
*Ruel "J R" Barbee, manager*
3924 Menaul Blvd NE
Albuquerque, NM 87110
505-837-2757

## La Paloma Bookshop
*Sandy Scott, owner*
308 W. Church St
Carlsbad, NM 88220
505-885-3542

**Lemstone Books**
Pat & Lyn Glennon, owners
Coronado Mall
Albuquerque, NM 87110
505-888-4656

**Logos of New Mexico**
Webb & Rickie Sherrill,
 managers
1636 Saint Michaels Dr
Santa Fe, NM 87501
505-473-0435

**Lovelines**
Judson Ray, owner
Broadmoor Shopping Center
1401 N. Turner
Hobbs, NM 88240
505-397-4336

**Oklahoma Adventist Book Center, Corrales Branch**
Laura Ward, manager
335 Academy Dr
Corrales, NM 87048
505-897-6799

**Rainbows & Sonshine**
Kathleen A. Shelton, owner
1321-C 18th St
Los Alamos, NM 87544
505-662-4484

**Son Life Bible & Gift**
Mary Starr Charlton, owner
1345-A Camino de Los Lopez
Santa Fe, NM 87505
505-471-9177
f: 505-471-9177

**Southwest Sales**
Mary Lou Rowley, owner
321 S. Avenue C
Portales, NM 88130
505-356-5223

**Sparrow Christian Bookstore**
Brenda Brunson, owner
419 W. Main
Artesia, NM 88210
505-748-3201

**Star of the Morning**
Howard De Witt, manager
1508 Tenth St
Alamagordo, NM 88310
505-434-0865

**Sunrise Bookstore (Mormon)**
Robert Smith, owner
7200 Menaul Blvd NE
Albuquerque, NM 87110
505-888-2634
f: 505-281-0151

## NATIONAL CHAINS

**Bookstar**
Kay Marcotte, manager
2201 Louisiana Blvd NE
Albuquerque, NM 87110
505-883-2644

**Book Warehouse**
Geoff Matthews, vice president,
 purchaser, buyer
Santa Fe Factory Stores,
 Suite B-200
8380 Cerrillos Road
Santa Fe, NM 87505
505-473-5508

**Borders Books & Music**
Diane Jones, manager
Winrock Mall, Suite 40
2100 Louisiana NE
Albuquerque, NM 87110
505-884-7711
f: 505-884-6435

## B. Dalton Bookseller

*Bruce Underwood, manager*
385 Coronado Center
Albuquerque, NM 87110
505-881-7757

**Branches:**
Cottonwood Mall
Albuquerque, NM 87125
Opens July 1996

North Plains Mall
N. Prince St & Manana Dr
Clovis, NM 88101
505-763-8311

## Hastings Books, Music & Video

**Branches:**
*David Hand, manager*
Security Center
1711 Tenth St
Alamagordo, NM 88310
505-437-2096

*Brian Dausses, manager*
Fair Plaza Shopping Center
6001-R Lomas Blvd NE
Albuquerque, NM 87110
505-266-1463

*Helen Taylor, manager*
Manzana Shopping Center
800 E. Juan Tabo NE
Albuquerque, NM 87120
505-296-6731

*Nevin Henderson, manager*
Montano Plaza
6100-F Coors Road NW
Albuquerque, NM 87120
505-898-5019

*Loretta Terrazas, manager*
Riverwalk Center
910 W. Pierce St
Carlsbad, NM 88220
505-887-7955

*David Hand, manager*
San Juan North
   Shopping Center
3000 E. 20th St
Farmington, NM 87401
505-327-3351

*Steve Juarez, manager*
Broadmoor Shopping Center,
   Space B
1401 N. Turner
Hobbs, NM 88240
505-393-3089

*Sylvia Rodriguez, manager*
Idaho Shopping Center
1300 S. El Paseo
Las Cruces, NM 88001
505-525-0023

*Bill Morey, manager*
Hilltop Plaza
   Shopping Center
1630 Rio Rancho Dr
Rio Rancho, NM 87124
505-892-3844

2801 N. Main
Roswell, NM 88201
505-622-6620

*Jim Rodgers, manager*
College Park South
2414 Cerrillos Road
Santa Fe, NM 87501
505-473-5788

## Hastings Multimedia Supercenter

La Miranda Shopping Center
4315 Wyoming NE
Albuquerque, NM 87109
505-299-7750

## Peace Craft

*Angelo Tomedi, chairperson*
*Laura Middlebrooks, director*
3107 Central Ave NE
Albuquerque, NM 87106
505-255-5229
f: 505-268-4234

Arts & crafts, Latin, cooking.

## Software Etc.

*Curt Babcock, manager*
Winrock Center, 72-A
2100 Louisiana Blvd NE
Albuquerque, NM 87110
505-888-9595

Computer software.

*Branches:*
Coronado Center
6600 Menaul NE
Albuquerque, NM 87110
505-860-8767

*Joe Bode, manager*
Villa Linda Mall, No. 1172
4250 Cerrillos Road
Santa Fe, NM 87505
505-474-4544

## Waldenbooks

*Kathy Izard, manager*
Coronado Center, Suite 61
6600 Menaul Blvd NE
Albuquerque, NM 87110
505-881-1584

*Branches:*
*Sondra Rouse, manager*
Animas Valley Mall
4601 E. Main
Farmington, NM 87401
505-327-7835

*Gayla Frame-Compos, manager*
Rio West
1300 W. I-40 Frontage Road
Gallup, NM 87301
505-722-7117

## Waldenbooks

*Janet Chapman manager*
Villa Linda Mall, Space 1434
4250 Cerrillos Road
Santa Fe, NM 87505
505-473-4050

# MAIL ORDER

## Abacus Books

*Robert F. Kadlec, owner*
1896 Lorca Dr
PO Box 6872
Santa Fe, NM 87502
505-471-2460

Antiquarian, books on books, Southwest.

## Adobe Booksellers

*Hy S. Adler, owner*
2416 Pennsylvania St NE
Albuquerque, NM 87110
505-299-1670

Southwest.

## Andre Dumont Maps & Books

*Andre Dumont, owner*
PO Box 10117
Santa Fe, NM 87504
505-986-9603
f: 505-986-6114

Antiquarian, cartography, Western, American exploration.

## Children's Book Corral

*Margery Valliant, owner*
1621 Park St SW
Albuquerque, NM 87104
505-765-1597

Spanish language, hardbound, mass-market paperback.

## Curiosity Books Inc.

*Stephanie Boutz, president*
1001 El Alhambra Circle NW
Albuquerque, NM 87107
505-343-0650
f: 505-343-0581

Successor to Cantwell's Books and Fine Papers. Special orders by phone and mail only.

## Le Gay Southwest Books

*L. E. & Mary R. Gay*
1023 Tierra Dr
Santa Fe, NM 87505
505-471-2393

Old & rare Arizoniana, New Mexicana, West Texas.

## High-Lonesome Books

*Cherie K. & M. H. Salmon*
PO Box 878
Silver City, NM 88062
505-388-3763

Western, sporting.

## Hyleana Fine Books

*Robert Dietz, owner*
6939 Edith Blvd NE
Albuquerque, NM 87113
t/f: 505-344-3410

Out-of-print Latin American, Southwest, third world, exploration.

## Jane Zwisohn Books

*Jane Zwisohn, owner*
524 Solano Dr NE
Albuquerque, NM 87108
505-255-4080

Antiquarian Latin American, travel, Western.

## Metaphysical Motivation Institute – Book Dept.

*Carmon Phillips, owner*
*Donna Bruss, manager*
641 Sudderth Dr
PO Drawer 400
Ruidoso, NM 88345
505-257-2811

Metaphysics.

## Paperback Previews

*Gypsy Kemp, owner*
PO Box 6781
Albuquerque, NM 87197
505-872-4461

General.

## Rocking A Books

*Anne C. Nagel, owner*
10312 Piedra Ct NW
Albuquerque, NM 87114
505-897-4433

Native American studies, Indian & Southwestern art.

## Richard Fitch Old Maps & Prints & Books

*Richard Fitch, owner*
2324 Calle Halcon
Santa Fe, NM 87505
505-982-2939
f: 505-982-3148

Antiquarian, cartography, Western, Canadian exploration.

## Skullduggery House Books

*Sharon Smith, owner, manager*
PO Box 1851
Alamagordo, NM 88311
505-434-6641
f: 505-437-5704

Mystery, detective, thriller.

## Spencer Maxwell Rare Books

Spencer Maxwell, owner
2600 W. Zia Road, Suite K-10
Santa Fe, NM 87505
505-474-4864

Antiquarian, Southwest, American Indian arts, Edward Abbey, Tony Hillerman.

## D. Turpen Books— Mexico & West

Donald C. Turpen, owner,
manager, buyer
PO Box 8736
Albuquerque, NM 87108
505-268-5323
f: 505-268-4527

Nonfiction, western, Mexican history.

## The Village Bookie

Mary Bradley, owner, manager
122-B Courseview Dr
PO Box 2615
Ruidoso, NM 88345
505-257-2904

Mystery, detective.

# INSTITUTIONS (Colleges, Museums)

## Albuquerque Academy Bookstore

Connie Johnson, manager
6400 Wyoming Blvd NE
Albuquerque, NM 87109
505-828-3217
f: 505-828-3320

College textbooks.

## Albuquerque TVI Bookstores

Sandra Rodman, director
525 Buena Vista SE
Albuquerque, NM 87106
505-224-3000
f: 505-224-4556

Careers, electronics, trades, fire science, building codes.

*Branch:*

Pat Madlener, manager
4700 Morris NE
Montoya Campus
Albuquerque, NM 87111
505-224-4510

## Aztec Ruins National Monument Bookstore

Barry Cooper, superintendent
Theresa Nichols, coordinator
Box 640, Ruins Rd
Aztec, NM 87410
505-334-6174
f: 505-334-6372

Archaeology, ethnic, natural history, Southwestern.

## Bandelier National Monument Bookstore

Linda Gaffney, manager
Albert Seidenkranz, liason
HCR 1, Box 1, Suite 2
Los Alamos, NM 87544
505-672-3861, ext. 515
f: 505-672-9607

Archaeology, New Mexicana, wildlife, horticulture, Bandelier National Monument, Native American.

## Capulin Volcano National Monument Bookstore

*Mary J. Karraker,*
*superintendent*
*Nancy Wizner, coordinator*
Visitor Center
Capulin, NM 88414
505-278-2201
f: 505-278-2211

Capulin volcano.

## Carlsbad Caverns Guadalupe Mountain Association

*Rick Labello, business manager*
PO Box 1417
Carlsbad, NM 88220
505-785-2318
f: 505-785-2333

Geology, natural history, bats, caves.

## Case Trading Post

*Robb Lucas, manager*
704 Camino Lejo
PO Box 5153
Santa Fe, NM 87502
505-982-4636
f: 505-989-7386

Native American studies, Southwest and Native American arts and crafts.

## Chaco Culture National Historical Park Bookstore

*Lawrence Belli, superintendent*
*Herschel Schulz, coordinator*
Star Rt 4, Box 6500
Bloomfield, NM 87413
505-786-7014
f: 505-986-7061 (call first)

Anthropology, archaeology, natural history, Chaco Canyon.

## Clovis Community College Campus Bookstore

*Jacques Ochs, manager*
417 Schepps Blvd
Clovis, NM 88101
505-769-2811
f: 505-769-4190

College textbooks.

## College of Santa Fe Bookstore

*Peggy Eaton, manager*
Saint Michael's Dr
Santa Fe, NM 87501
505-473-0812

Southwest, college texts.

## College of the Southwest Bookstore

*Bennetta Seymore, manager*
6610 Lovington Hwy
Hobbs, NM 88240
505-392-6561
f: 505-392-6006

College textbooks.

## Communications Media Ojo de Dios

*Colleen Olinger, manager*
Science Museum Complex
15th & Central
Los Alamos, NM 87544
505-662-9589
f: 505-662-3713

Southwest, sci-tech, science trade.

## Eastern New Mexico University Bookstore

*John Wilson, manager, buyer*
Station 14
Portales, NM 88130
505-562-2721
f: 505-562-2716

College textbooks.

### Branch:

*Gloria Fresquez, manager*
Roswell Campus
52-A University Blvd
Roswell, NM 88202
505-624-7194
f: 505-624-7119

## El Malpais National Monument

*Leslie DeLong, coordinator*
*Ken Mabery, alternate*
620 E. Santa Fe Ave
Grants, NM 87020
505-285-4641
f: 505-285-5661

Natural history, volcanology, cultural history, children's, field guides.

## El Morro National Monument Bookstore

*Michelle Pelletier,*
*superintendent*
*Thomas C. Townley,*
*coordinator*
Route 2, Box 43
Ramah, NM 87321
505-783-4226
f: 505-783-4689

El Morro National Monument.

## Fort Union National Monument Bookstore

*Harry Myers, superintendent*
*Frank Torres, coordinator*
Watrous, NM 87753
505-425-8025
f: 505-454-1155 (call first)

Fort Union, frontier military history, Santa Fe Trail.

## Gila Cliff Dwellings National Monument

*Doug Thompson and*
*Virginia Chute, coordinators*
Route 11, Box 100
Silver City, NM 88061
505-536-9461
t/f: 505-536-9344 (call first)

New Mexicana, travel, natural history, environment, Southwest history, prehistory.

## Kit Carson Home & Museum Book Dept.

*R. C. Gordon-McCutchan,*
*superintendent, buyer*
Old Kit Carson Road
Drawer CCC
Taos, NM 87571
505-758-4741
f: 505-758-0330

New Mexicana, Native American, Southwest, fur trade.

## Los Alamos Historical Society Museum Shop

*Diane Pfaff, manager*
1921 Jupiter
PO Box 43
Los Alamos, NM 87544
505-662-4493

Southwest, history of Los Alamos and the atomic bomb.

## Maxwell Museum Store

*Catherine Baudoin, manager*
University of New Mexico
Albuquerque, NM 87131
505-277-8601
f: 505-277-1547

Anthropology, archaeology, Native American, Southwest.

## Millicent Rogers Museum Bookshop

*Carmela Duran, manager*
Museum Road
PO Box A
Taos, NM 87571
505-758-4316
f: 505-758-5751

Southwest, Native American, Spanish history and literature, art of Taos.

*Branch:*

*Melody Gladin-Kehoe, manager*
Taos Plaza
115 E. McCarthy Dr
Taos, NM 87571
505-751-0808

## Museum of New Mexico Foundation Shops

*Anna Burgess, manager*
Palace of the Governors
PO Box 2065
Santa Fe, NM 87504
505-982-3016
f: 505-982-7253

Fine arts, folklore, New Mexicana, Southwest, Native American arts and crafts.

## National College Bookstore

*Lisa Knigge, director*
1202 Pennsylvania Ave NE
Albuquerque, NM 87110
t: 505-265-7517
f: 505-265-7542

Business, management, computer science.

## Navajo Community College Bookstore

*Leroy Begay, manager*
PO Box 580
Shiprock, NM 87420
505-368-5291, ext. 237
f: 505-368-5481

College textbooks, arts and crafts, Navajo history, Native American literature.

## New Mexico Institute of Mining & Technology Bookstore

*Elaine Torres, manager*
Student Union, Campus Station
Socorro, NM 87801
505-835-5415

Geology, physics, sci-tech, astronomy.

## New Mexico Junior College Bookstore

Mark Freed, manager
5317 Lovington Hwy
Hobbs, NM 88240
505-392-4510
f: 505-392-2391

College textbooks.

## New Mexico State University Bookstore

Ron Benson
Corbett Center, New Mexico
    State University
Las Cruces, NM 88003
505-646-7660

General, college, used textbooks.

## NMSU – Alamagordo Branch Bookstore

Doris Wright, manager
PO Box 477
Alamagordo, NM 88310
505-439-3606
f: 505-439-3643

Computer science, government publications, history, philosophy, science fiction.

## NMSU – Carlsbad Branch Bookstore

Carolyn Davis, manager
1500 University Dr
Carlsbad, NM 88220
505-885-8831

College textbooks.

## Northern New Mexico Community College Bookstore

Mary A. Garcia, manager
1002 N. Paseo Onate
PO Box 2053
Española, NM 87532
505-753-7141

Southwest, college.

## Otowi Station

Colleen Olinger, owner
1350 Central
Los Alamos, NM 87544
505-662-9589

General, technical.

## Pecos National Historic Park Bookstore

Ann Rasor and John Loleit,
    coordinators
Drawer 418
Pecos, NM 87552
505-757-6032
f: 505-757-8460

Natural history, Southwest, anthropology, fiction, history.

## Petroglyph National Monument

Stephen E. Whitesell,
    superintendent
Mardi Butt, coordinator
4735 Atrisco NW
Albuquerque, NM 87120
505-839-4429
f: 505-768-3817

Petroglyph National Monument, related subjects.

## Roswell Museum & Art Center Bookstore

*Elaine French, manager, buyer*
11th St & Main
Roswell, NM 88201
505-624-6744
f: 505-624-6785

Art, history, Southwest, sci-tech, fine arts.

## Saint John's College Bookstore

*Andrea D'Amato, manager, buyer*
Camino de Cruz Blanca
Santa Fe, NM 87501
505-984-6056
f: 505-984-6026

Class studies, religion, philosophy, physical science.

## Salinas Pueblo Missions National Monument

*James Boll and Loretta Silva, coordinators*
Ripley & Broadway
PO Box 496
Mountainair, NM 87036
505-847-2585
f: 505-847-2441

Southwest, Native American pueblos, prehistory of area, 17th-century mission church.

## Santa Fe Community College Bookstore

*LeeAnn Martinez, manager*
PO Box 4187
Santa Fe, NM 87502
505-471-8200
f: 505-438-1237

College textbooks, Spanish language.

## San Juan College Bookstore

*Kim Decker, manager*
4601 College Blvd
Farmington, NM 87402
505-599-0286
f: 505-599-0385

College textbooks.

## Southwest Natural Cultural Heritage Association

*Lisa D. Madsen, executive director*
*Stephen G. Maurer, manager*
*Jeff Honker, buyer*
Drawer E
Albuquerque, NM 87103
505-345-9168
f: 505-344-1543

Natural history.

## University of New Mexico Bookstore

*Stephanie Richardson*
University of New Mexico
Yale Mall
Albuquerque, NM 87131
505-277-5451
800-981-2665
f: 505-277-8665

General, college, used textbooks.

*Branch:*

*Marian Scanland, manager*
North Campus
Albuquerque, NM 87131
505-277-5827

## University of New Mexico Art Museum Shop

Chris Squire, *manager*
Fine Arts Center, No. 1017
Albuquerque, NM 87131
505-277-4001
f: 505-277-7315

Art, exhibition catalogs.

## University of New Mexico Gallup Campus Bookstore

Bill Hockensmith, *manager*
200 College Road
Gallup, NM 87301
505-863-7586
f: 505-863-7644

Navajo language.

## University of Phoenix Bookstore

Marcial Sanchez, *manager*
7471 Pan American Fwy NE
Albuquerque, NM 87109
505-821-4800
f: 505-821-5551

College textbooks.

## Western New Mexico University Bookstore

Jean Springler, *director*
1000 W. College Ave
PO Box 72
Silver City, NM 88062
505-538-6123
f: 505-538-6123

College textbooks, local authors, local history, reference, Southwest history.

## White Sands National Monument Bookstore

Yvonne Taylor, *manager*
19955 Hwy 70
PO Box 1086
Holloman AFB
Alamagordo, NM 88330
505-479-4333
f: 505-479-4333

White Sands National Monument, natural history, NM history.

# Distributors & Wholesalers

**A**ccording to our current information, there is but one resident general book distributor in New Mexico (Gannon). However, regional distributors such as Treasure Chest and Sunbelt also take an interest in books produced in and about New Mexico. We have included also the major national book jobbers, Ingram Book Company (which presently dominates the market) and Baker & Taylor, as well as a few specialty distributors such as Quality Books (libraries) and New Leaf (New Age, spirituality, healing).

A book "distributor" may be merely a jobber, wholesaling books to retailers while leaving the marketing and publicity efforts to the publisher. Others may take a more active role in supporting a publisher's books, which might include catalogs, joint mailings, participation in shows, etc. Some publishers, such as Johnson Books of Boulder, Colorado, market and distribute the books of compatible publishers. Before signing an agreement with a distributor, you should find out what the firm will and won't do, investigate costs and discounts, and negotiate an arrangement that works for you financially.

### Gannon Distributing Company

*Robert Sheldon,*
*managing director*
*Phil Potter, sales manager*
2887 Cooks Road
Santa Fe, NM 87505
505-438-3430, 800-442-2044
f: 505-471-5916

Wholesaler of Southwestern and Native American books, bestsellers and sidelines.

### Baker & Taylor Books

*Eleanor Fanicase*
*Julia Quinones*
652 E. Main St
Bridgewater, NJ 08807
908-218-0400

Known formerly as the largest national distributor to libraries, now serves bookstores as well.

### Blackwell North America

100 University Court
Blackwood, NJ 08012
609-228-8900

Distributor to libraries.

### Bookbuilders West

PO Box 7046
San Francisco, CA 94120
415-273-5790

### Bookpeople

7900 Edgewater Drive
Oakland, CA 94621
510-632-4700
f: 510-632-1281

Major independent press consignment distributor.

### The Book House, Inc.

208 W. Chicago
Jonesville, MI 49250
517-849-2117

Distributor to libraries.

### Brodart, Co.

500 Arch St
Williamsport, PA 17705
717-326-2401

Distributor to libraries.

### De Vorss & Co.

1046 Princeton Dr
PO Box 550
Marina del Ren, CA 90294
213-870-7478
f: 310-821-6290

Spiritual, occult and New Age titles. Very selective.

### Ingram Book Company

*David Quinn, buyer*
11333 East 53rd Ave
Denver CO 80239
303-375-7240, 800-973-8000
f: 303-375-7241

*National headquarters:*
1 Ingram Blvd
La Vergne, TN 37086
615-793-5000
f: 615-793-5655

Largest general trade book distributor in the known universe; has dominated book distribution in the United States for the past several years.

### Midwest Library Service

11443 St. Charles Rock Rd
Bridgeton, MO 63044
314-739-3100
f: 314-739-1326

Distributor to libraries.

## New Leaf Distributing

*Halim Provo-Thompson*
401 Thornton Road
Lithia Springs, GA 30057
770-948-7845

The major national distributor of New Age, health and alternative healing, and spiritual books to bookstores.

## Pacific Pipeline, Inc.

*Dennis Zook, Bill Preston*
8030 South 228th St
Kent WA 98032
206-872-5523
f: 206-244-6109

Largest independent book wholesaler on the West Coast; Western regional subjects.

## Quality Books, Inc.

*Michael Huston*
1003 W. Pines Road
Oregon, IL 61061
815-732-4450
f: 815-732-4499

Distributes selected small press books to libraries.

## Sunbelt Publications

*Lowell Lindsay*
1250 Fayette Street
El Cajon, CA 92020
619-258-4911
f: 619-258-4916

Distributes regional books from regional publishers; main focus is West Coast.

## Treasure Chest Publications, Inc.

PO Box 5250
Tucson, AZ 85703
602-623-9558, 800-969-9558
f: 602-624-5888

Publisher of Southwestern topics that distributes books for other regional publishers.

## Unique Books, Inc.

*Richard Capps*
4320 Grove Ave
Gurnee, IL 60031
708-623-9171
f: 708-623-7238

Distributes independently published books to libraries in the U.S. and Canada.

# Libraries in New Mexico

**T**his list includes, we hope, all public as well as institutional (college, Native American, military, prison, museum, etc.) libraries in the state of New Mexico, in most cases with the name of the director or head librarian. Libraries listed range from the Albuquerque Public Library with its many branches to those that serve New Mexico's smallest communities, such as the Village of Reserve Library, Magdalena Public Library, and the David Cargo Public Library in Mora.

Libraries and librarians in the state are supported by the New Mexico Library Association, New Mexico Library Foundation, New Mexico State Library, and the New Mexico Center for the Book (see *Book Related Organizations*). Libraries are increasingly positioning themselves as information centers, with OCLC computer links to libraries across the country, computerized cataloging and interlibrary loans, and public access to the

## Alamagordo Public Library

*Paul Miller, director*
920 Oregon Ave
Alamogordo, NM 88310
505-439-4240
f: 505-439-4141

## Albert W. Thompson Memorial Library

*Lacey Cook, librarian*
17 Chestnut St
Clayton, NM 88415
505-374-9423
f: 505-374-8497

## Albuquerque Museum Library

*James Moore, museum director*
PO Box 1293
Albuquerque, NM 87103
505-243-7244

## Albuquerque Public Library / Main Library

*Joe Sabatini, head*
501 Copper NW
Albuquerque, NM 87102
505-768-5140
f: 505-768-5185

## APL / East Mountain Branch

*Toni Osburn, manager*
1 Old Tijeras Rd
Tijeras, NM 87059
505-281-8508

## APL / Erna Fergusson Branch

*Sandra Masson, manager*
3700 San Mateo Blvd NE
Albuquerque, NM 87110
505-888-8100

## APL / Ernie Pyle Branch

900 Girard Blvd SE
Albuquerque, NM 87106
505-256-2065

## APL / Esperanza Branch

*Mary Lou Sulllenberger, manager*
5600 Esperanza Dr NW
Albuquerque, NM 87105
505-836-0684

## APL / Juan Tabo Branch

*Joani Murphy, manager*
3407 Juan Tabo Blvd NE
Albuquerque, NM 87111
505-291-6260

## APL / Lomas-Tramway Branch

*Toni Osburn, manager*
908 Eastridge Dr NE
Albuquerque, NM 87123
505-291-6295

## APL / Los Griegos Branch

*Julie Denning, manager*
1000 Griegos Rd NE
Albuquerque, NM 87107
505-761-4020

## APL / San Pedro Branch

*Stephanie Egar, manager*
5600 Trumbull Ave SE
Albuquerque, NM 87108
505-256-2067

## APL / South Broadway Branch

*Robert Martinez, manager*
1025 Broadway Blvd SE
Albuquerque, NM 87102
505-764-1742

## APL / Taylor Ranch Branch

Mary Lou Sullenberger, manager
5700 Bogart St NW
Albuquerq..e, NM 87120
505-897-8816

## Albuquerque Technical Vocational Institute Library

Jacque Buckhanan, circulation
Main Campus
525 Buena Vista SE
Albuquerque, NM 87106
505-224-3274
f: 505-224-3293

## Angel Fire Community Library

Ruth Lawrence, librarian
1 North Angel Fire Road
Angel Fire, NM 87710
505-377-3511

## Archdiocese Library

4000 St Joseph's Place NW
Albuquerque, NM 87120
505-831-8129

## Archdiocese Library

Marina Ochoa, librarian
223 Cathedral Place
Santa Fe, NM 87501
505-983-3811

## Armand Hammer United World College of the American West

Dorothy Meredith, librarian
PO Box 248
Santa Fe, NM 87731
505-454-1461

## Artesia Public Library

Pamela Castle, librarian
306 W Richardson
Artesia, NM 88210
505-746-4252

## Arthur Johnson Memorial Library

Richard Azar, librarian
44 Cook Ave
Raton, NM 87440
505-445-9711
f: 505-455-3398

## Aztec Public Library

Kathi Browning, librarian
201 W Chaco
Aztec, NM 87410-1996
505-334-9456
f: 505-334-3586

## Bayard Public Library

Ernestine Camp, librarian
Drawer T
Bayard, NM 88023
505-537-6244
f: 505-537-5271

## Belen Public Library

Dolores Padilla, librarian
333 Becker Ave
Belen, NM 87002
505-864-7797
f: 505-864-7522

## Bloomfield Community Library

Esther Trost, librarian
PO Box 1839
Bloomfield, NM 87413
505-632-8315
f: 505-632-2278

## Bosque Farms Community Library

*Barbara Moore, librarian*
1455 West Bosque Loop
Bosque Farms, NM 87068
505-869-2227

## Cannon Air Force Base/ Library FL 4855

*Marsha Dreier, librarian*
Cannon Air Force Base,
    NM 88103
505-784-2786

## Carlsbad Caverns National Park Library

*Barbara Bilbo, librarian*
3225 National Parks Highway
Carlsbad, NM 88220
505-885-8884

## Carlsbad Public Library

*Beverly McFarland, director*
101 S. Halagueno St
Carlsbad, NM 88220
505-885-0731
f: 505-885-8809

## Carnegie Public Library

*Ann Kaiser, librarian*
500 National Ave
Las Vegas, NM 87701
505-454-1401

## Center for Anthropological Studies Library

PO Box 14576
Albuquerque, NM 87191
505-296-4836

## Center for SW Research

505-277-7171
cswrref@unm.edu

## Central NM Correctional Facility Library

*Andrew Breland, librarian*
PO Drawer 1328
1525 Morris Rd SW
Los Lunas, NM 87031
505-865-1622
f: 505-865-2316

## Clovis-Carver Public Library

*Sandy White, director*
701 Main St
Clovis, NM 88101
505-769-7840
f:505-769-7842

## Clovis Community College Library

*Deborah McBeth, librarian*
417 Schepps Blvd
Clovis, NM 88101
505-769-4080

## College of Santa Fe Fogelson Library

1600 Saint Michaels Dr
Santa Fe, NM 87505
505-473-6576
f: 505-473-6593

## College of the Southwest/ Scarborough Memorial Library

*John McCance, librarian*
6610 Lovington Highway
Hobbs, NM 88240
505-392-6561
f: 505-392-6006

### Corrales Community Library

*Carla Spencer, librarian*
PO Drawer L
Corrales, NM 87048
505-897-0733
f: 505-897-0596

### Crownpoint Institute of Technology Library

*Lee E. Platero, librarian*
PO Drawer K
Crownpoint, NM 87313
505-786-5851

### Cuba Community Library

Route 126, PO Box 426
Cuba, NM 87013
505-289-3100
f: 505-289-3769

### David Cargo Public Library

*Ruth Foyt, librarian*
PO Box 638
Mora, NM 87732
505-387-5029

### Dona Ana Community College

*Jennifer Minter,*
  *library coordinator*
3400 S. Espina St
Las Cruces, NM 88003
505-527-7555
f: 505-527-7515

### Eastern NM University Roswell Learning Resource Center

*Rollah Aston, director*
P. O. Box 6000
Roswell, NM 88202
505-624-7282
f: 505-624-7119

### Edgewood Community Library

*Anne Dacey-Lucas, librarian*
PO Box 1134
Edgewood, NM 87015
505-281-0138
f: 505-281-0138

### El Rito Public Library

*Jane Kramer, librarian*
PO Box 5
El Rito, NM 87530
505-581-4789
f: 505-581-5608

### Española Public Library

*Marilyn Reeves, director*
314-A Onate St NW
Espanola, NM 87532
505-753-3860
f: 505-753-2523

### Estancia Public Library

10th & Highland
PO Box 68
Estancia, NM 87016
505-384-2708

### Esther Bone Memorial Library

PO Box 15670
950 Pinetree Rd SE
Rio Rancho, NM 87124
505-891-7244
f: 505-891-7246

### Eunice Public Library

*Peggy Suter, librarian*
10th and N Streets
PO Box 1629
Eunice, NM 88231
505-394-2336
f: 505-394-360

## Farmington Public Library

*Kathy Wilson,*
*library administrator*
100 West Broadway
Farmington, NM 87401
505-599-1270
f: 505-599-0381

## Farmington Public Library East

2702 E. 22nd
Farmington, NM 87401
505-599-1291

## Fort Sumner Public Library

*Karla Hunt, librarian*
300 W. Sumner
Drawer D
Fort Sumner, NM 88119
505-355-2832
f: 505-355-7732

## Fred Macaron Library

*Annie Nordman, librarian*
PO Box 726
Springer, NM 87747
505-483-2848
f: 505-483-2670

## Ghost Ranch Library

*Edgar W. Davy, librarian*
Ghost Ranch
Conference Center
HC 77, Box 11
Abiquiu, NM 87510
505-685-4333
f: 505 685-4519

## Glenwood Community Library

*Pepper LeBlanc, librarian*
PO Box 144
Glenwood, NM 88039
505-539-2686

## Hagerman Community Library

*Ditta McCullough, librarian*
209 E. Argyle
PO Box 247
Hagerman, NM 88232
505-752-3204

## Hatch Public Library

PO Box 289
503 E. Hall
Hatch, NM 87937
505-267-5132

## Hispanic Culture Foundation

*Carol Guzman, librarian*
PO Box 7279
Albuquerque, NM 87194

## Hobbs Public Library

*Cris Adams, librarian*
509 N. Shipp
Hobbs, NM 88240
505-397-9328

## Holloman Air Force Base/ Library FL 4801

*Cora Austin, Library director*
955 First St, Bldg 205
Holloman, NM 88330
505-479-3939
f: 505-475-5340

## Institution of American Indian Arts Library

*Allen Schwartz, librarian*
PO Box 20007
Santa Fe, NM 87504
505-988-6423
f: 505 988-6446

## Instructional Resource Center

Sara Mitchell, contact
PO Box 19000
Clovis, NM 88101
505-769-4520

## Intel Corp-F9-53

Mary Frances Campana,
   contact
4100 Sara Road
Rio Rancho, NM 87124
505-893-7000

## Isleta Pueblo Library

Ulysses Abeita, librarian
Resource Center
PO Box 1270
Isleta, NM 87022
505-869-2597
f: 505-869-4236

## Jemez Pueblo Community Library

Judy Asbury, contact
PO Box 9
Jemez, NM 87024
505-834-9171

## Jemez Springs Community Library

Susan Minter, librarian
PO Box 247
Jemez Springs, NM 87025

## Jicarilla Library

Rose Vigil, librarian
PO Box 507
Dulce, NM 87528
505-759-3616
f: 505-759-3492

## Kenneth Schlientz Memorial Library

Clara Rey, librarian
602 S. Second St
Tucumcari, NM 88401
505-461-0295
f: 505-461-0297

## Kit Carson Memorial Foundation Historical Research Library

PO Drawer B
Taos, NM 87571
505-758-4741

## Los Alamos County Library

Mary Pat Kraemer, director
2400 Central Ave
Los Alamos, NM 87544
505-662-8240
f: 505 662-8245

## LACL / White Rock Branch

Carol-lee McKenna, director
133 Longview Drive
White Rock, NM 87544
505-662-8265

## Los Alamos National Laboratory Library

Richard Luce, director
PO Box 1663, MS P362
Los Alamos, NM 87545
505-667-4448
f: 505 665-2948
web site:
   http://lid.www.lanl.gov

## Los Lunas Community Library

*Carmen Jaramillo, librarian*
PO Box 1209
460 Main St
Los Lunas, NM 87031
505-865-6779
f: 505 865-6063

## Los Lunas Correctional Center Library

*Sandra Yeffa, contact*
3201 Highway 85 SW
Los Lunas, NM 87031
505-865-2732
f: 505 865-6063

## Lovington Public Library

*Mary Lee Smith, director*
115 S. Main
Lovington, NM 88260
505-396-3144
f: 505 396-7189

## Luna Vocational- Technical Institute Learning Resource Center

*Margaret Maestas-Armijo, director*
PO Box 300
Las Vegas, NM 87701
505 454-2500
f: 505 454-2518

## Magdalena Public Library

*Kitty Martin, librarian*
PO Box 86
Magdalena, NM 87825
505 854-2261

## Martha Liebert Library

829 Camino del Pueblo
PO Box 10
Bernalillo, NM 87004
505-867-3311
f: 505-867-0481

## Menaul Historical Library of the SW

301 Menaul Blvd NE
Albuquerque, NM 87107
505-345-7727

## Mesa Technical College Library

824 West Hines Ave
Tucumcari, NM 88401
505-461-4413
f: 505-461-1901

## Millicent Rogers Museum Library

*Guadalupe Tafoya, acting director*
PO Box A
Taos, NM 87571
505-758-2462
f: 505-758-5751

## Moriarty Community Library

*Wanda Tritt, librarian*
PO Box 1917
Moriarty, NM 87035
505-832-6919
f: 505-832-6919

## Mother Whiteside Memorial Library

*Jae Luree King, librarian*
525 West High St
Grants, NM 87020
505-287-7927
f: 505 287-4793

## Mountainair Civic Library

Joan Bourke, librarian
110 N. Roosevelt
Mountainair, NM 87036
505-847-2450

## Museum of Fine Arts Library

Mary Jebsen, director
107 W. Palace Ave
PO Box 2087
Santa Fe, NM 87504
505-827-4453

## Museum of Indian Arts and Culture / Laboratory of Anthropology Library

Laura Holt, librarian
PO Box 2087
Santa Fe, NM 87504
505-827-6344
f: 505-827-6497

## Museum of International Folk Art Library

Judy Sellers, librarian
PO Box 2087
Santa Fe, NM 87504

## Museum of New Mexico History Library

Orlando Romero, librarian
110 Washington Ave
PO Box 2087
Santa Fe, NM 87504
505-827-6470

## National Atomic Museum Library

Diana Zepeda, librarian
PO Box 5400
Albuquerque, NM 87185
505-845-4378

## National Solar Observatory Technical Library

John Cornett, librarian
Sunspot, NM 88349
505-434-1390

## Native American Studies Library

Alison Freese, librarian
1812 Las Lomas NE
Albuquerque, NM 87131
505-277-3917
f: 505-277-1818

## Navajo Community College

Eleanor K. Guenther, librarian
PO Box 580
Shiprock, NM 87420
505-368-5291

## Navajo Community College Library

Edith Landau, librarian
Tsaile, Arizona 86556
520-724-6133

## Navajo Nation Library

Irving Nelson, Program director
PO Box 9040
Window Rock, AZ 86515
520-871-6376
f: 520-871-7304

## NM Coalition for Literacy's Literary Resource Center

PO Box 6085
Santa Fe, NM 87502
505-982-3997
1-800-233-7587
f: 505-982-4095

## NM Junior College Pannell Library

*Randall Gaylor, librarian*
5317 Lovington Highway
Hobbs, NM 88240
505-392-5473
f: 505-392-2527

## NM Legislative Council Service Library

Santa Fe, NM 87503
505-986-4600
f: 505-986-4610

## NM Museum of Natural History Library

*Susan Cowan, contact*
1801 Mountain Rd
Albuquerque, NM 87104
505-841-8837

## NM School for the Deaf

*Carla Fenner, librarian*
1060 Cerrillos Rd
Santa Fe, NM 87501
505-827-6743

## NM School for the Visually Handicapped

*Kathy Flanary, librarian*
1900 N. White Sands Blvd
Alamogordo, NM 88310
505-437-3505

## NM State Library

*Karen Watkins, state librarian*
325 Don Gaspar Ave
Santa Fe, NM 87501
505-827-3800, 800-759-7687
f: 505-827-3888

## NM Women's Correctional Facility

*Memory Thorn, librarian*
PO Box 800
Grants, NM 87020
505-287-7961

## NMSU Alamogordo/ David H. Townsend Library

*Stanley Ruckman, director*
PO Box 477
2400 N. Scenic Drive
Alamogordo, NM 88310
505-439-3650
f: 505-439-3657

## NMSU Library / Branson

PO Box 30006
Las Cruces, NM 88003
505-646-3101
f: 505-646-7477

## NMSU Library/ Carlsbad

*Julia White, librarian*
1500 University Drive
Carlsbad, NM 88220
505-885-8831
f: 505-885-4951

## NMSU Library/ Grants

*Frederic H. Wilding-White, librarian*
1500 Third St
Grants, NM 87020
505-287-7981
f: 505 287-7992

## NMSU Library/ New

PO Box 30006
Las Cruces, NM 88003
505-646-6910
f: 505 646-4335

## Northern NM Community College Library

*Isabe Rodarte, director*
1002 Onate
Espanola, NM 87532
505-747-2241
f: 505 747-2245

**Octavia Fellin Public Library**
*Mary Browder, director*
115 W. Hill Rd
Gallup, NM 87301
505-863-1291
f: 505-863-9352

**Onate Center Library**
*Estevan Arellano, contact*
PO Box 1256
Espanola, NM 87532
505-852-4639

**Parks College Library**
*Rau Herrera, contact*
1023 Tijeras NW
Albuquerque, NM 87102
505-843-7500

**Penitentiary of NM Library**
*Barbara Gordon, librarian*
Box 1059
Santa Fe, NM 87504
505-827-7332

**Philmont Museum/ Seton Memorial Library**
*Annette Carlisle, librarian*
Philmont Scout Ranch, NM 87714
505-376-2281

**Pojoaque Pueblo Community Library**
*Jacqualine Nielsen, librarian*
Route ll, Box 71
Santa Fe, NM 87501
505-455-7511

**Portales Public Library**
*Denise Burnett, director*
218 S. Avenue B
Portales, NM 88130
505-356-3940
f: 505 356-3964

**Pueblo de Cochiti Community Library**
*Amy Suina, librarian*
PO Box 153
Cochiti Pueblo, NM 87072
505-465-2244

**Pueblo of Laguna Library**
*Elizabeth Wacondo, librarian*
PO Box 194
Laguna Pueblo, NM 87026
505-552-6280
f: 505-243-9636

**Red River Public Library**
*Kerry Shepherd, librarian*
Box 1020
Red River, NM 87558
505-754-6564

**Rehobeth Veenstra Memorial Library**
*Jenny Tamminga, contact*
Box 41
Rehobeth, NM 87322
505-863-4412

**Rio Grande Valley Library System**
*Alan Clark, director*
501 Copper NW
Albuquerque, NM 87102
505-768-5100
f: 505-768-5191

**Roswell Museum and Art Center Library**
*Dawn Selter, librarian*
100 W. 11th St
Roswell, NM 88201
505-624-6744

**Roswell Public Library**
*Betty Long, director*
301 N. Pennsylvania Ave
Roswell, NM 88201
505-622-3400
f: 505-622-7107

**Ruidoso Public Library**
*Nancy Eckert, director*
501 Junction Rd
Box 3539
Ruidoso, NM 88345
505-257-4335
f: 505-257-5994

**San Felipe Pueblo Library**
PO Box 4339
San Felipe Pueblo, NM 87001
505-867-5234

**San Ildefonso Pueblo Community Library**
*Irene Tse-pe, librarian*
Route 5 Box 315A
San Ildefonso Pueblo,
   NM 87501
505-455-2424

**San Juan College Library**
4601 College Blvd
Farmington, NM 87402
505-599-0249
f: 505 599-0385

**San Juan County Museum Salmon Ruin Library**
*Mathew Smith, contact*
PO Box 125
Bloomfield, NM 87413
505-632-2013
f: 505-632-1707

**Santa Fe Public Library/ Administration**
*Joanne Werger, director*
145 Washington Ave
Santa Fe, NM 87501
505-984-6789
f: 505-984-6676

**Santa Fe Public Library / Main Library**
*Valerie Brooker, director*
145 Washington Ave
Santa Fe, NM 87501
505-984-6780

**SFPL / Oliver LaFarge Branch**
*Bruce Adams, director*
1730 Llano St
Santa Fe, NM 87505
505-473-7260
f: 505 473-7261

**Santa Domingo Library**
*Doreen Bird, librarian*
PO Box 99
Santo Domingo Pueblo,
NM 87052

**School of American Research Library**
*Jane Gillentine, librarian*
PO Box 2188
660 Garcia St
Santa Fe, NM 87504
505-984-2177

## Socorro Public Library

Lucie Olson, librarian
401 Park St
Socorro, NM 87801
505-835-1114
f: 505-835-1182

## Southern NM Correctional Facility Library

PO Box 639
Las Cruces, NM 88004
505-523-3200
f: 505-524-7859

## Southwestern College Quimby Memorial Library

Mary Jebsen, librarian
PO Box 4788
Santa Fe, NM 87502
505-471-5756

## Southwestern Indian Polytechnic Institute Library

Paula M. Smith, librarian
PO Box 10146
Albuquerque, NM 87102
505-897-5352

## Space Center / Teacher–Student Resource Center

Jackie Diehl, librarian
PO Box 533
Alamogordo, NM 88311
505-437-2840

## St John's College Meem Library

Inga M. Waite, librarian
1160 Camino Cruz Blanca
Santa Fe, NM 87501
505-984-6041
f: 505-989-9269

## State Records and Archives

Elaine Olah, director
404 Montezuma St
Santa Fe, NM 87505
505-827-7332

## Supreme Court Law Library

Thaddeus Bejnar, librarian
237 Don Gaspar Ave
PO Drawer L
Santa Fe, NM 87504
505-827-4850
f: 505-827-4852

## Taos Public Library

Tracy McCallum, director
402 Camino de la Placita
Taos, NM 87571
505-758-3063
f: 505-758-7864

## Tatum Community Library

Sandra Herrera, contact
216 E. Broadway
PO Box 156
Tatum, NM 88267
505-398-4822
f: 505-398-4823

## The Public Library

Margaret Costales, director
515 College Ave
Silver City, 88061
505-538-3672
f: 505-538-5123

## Thomas Branigan Memorial Library

Carol Brey, library director
200 E. Picacho Ave
Las Cruces, NM 88001
505-526-1047
f: 505-527-6181

## Truth or Consequences Public Library

*Ellanie Sampson, librarian*
25 Library Lane
Truth or Consequences,
    NM 87901
505-894-3027
f: 505-894-2068

## University of New Mexico General Library

*Susan Deese-Roberts, director*
Albuquerque, NM 87131
505-277-4241
f: 505-277-6019

## UNM School of Law Library

1117 Stanford NE
Albuquerque, NM 87106
505-277-6236
f: 505-277-0068

## UNM Spanish Resource Center

*Blanca Sagarna, director*
4125 Carlisle Blvd NE
Albuquerque, NM 87107
505-277-3696
f: 505-277-5096

## UNM / Taos Campus

*Steve Torma, librarian*
115 Civic Plaza Drive
Taos, NM 87571
Phone 505-751-4357

## UNM / Valencia Campus

*Kris Warmoth, librarian*
280 La Entrada
Los Lunas, NM 87031
505-865-1630

## UNM / Gallup Campus Zollinger Library

*Charles Current, librarian*
200 College Rd
Gallup, NM 87301
505-863-7500

## US National Park Service SW Regional Office Library

*Amalin Ferguson, librarian*
PO Box 728
1220 S. St Francis Drive
Santa Fe, NM 87504
505-988-6840
f: 505-988-6876

## Valley Community Library

*Katie Bliss, librarian*
PO Box 1476
136 Anthony Drive
Anthony, NM 88021
505-822-5946

## Village of Reserve Library

*Elaine Freshour, librarian*
PO Box 587
505-533-6276

## Western NM Correctional Facility Library

PO Drawer 250
Grants, NM 87020
505-287-7961
f: 505-287-7558

## Western NM University/ Miller Library

PO Box 680
Siver City, NM 88062
505-538-6350
f: 505-538-6178

### Wheelright Museum Library

*Keltah Narbutovskih, librarian*
PO Box 5153
Santa Fe, NM 87502
505-982-4636

### WSMR Post Library

*Rita L. Smith, director*
Building 464
White Sands Missile Range,
   NM 88002
505-678-5820
f: 505-678-1556

### Woolworth Community Library

3rd and Utah
Jal, NM 88252
505-395-3268
f: 505-395-2138
f/m: 800-748-2138

### Zimmerman Library

*Robert Migeault, dean*
University of New Mexico
Albuquerque, NM 87131
505-277-5761
f: 505-277-6019

### Zuni Public Library

*Cordelia Hooee, librarian*
PO Box 339
Zuni Pueblo, NM 87327
505-782-5630
f: 505-782-2700

# Literacy Programs in
# New Mexico

 **B**asic ability to read in New Mexico's communities is supported by volunteer groups such as chapters of the Literacy Volunteers of America (LVA), private non-profit programs such as the Home Education Livelihood Program (HELP) which serves migrant populations, local government agencies, libraries, and Adult Basic Education (ABE) programs in the colleges.

The New Mexico Coalition for Literacy, which provided this list, functions as an information and support clearinghouse for these many local services. Contact Michelle Jaschke, executive director, New Mexico Coalition for Literacy, P.O. Box 6085, Santa Fe, NM 87502, 505-982-3997 (or toll-free statewide: 800-233-7587).

# ADULT BASIC EDUCATION

*When contacting these programs, be sure to include Adult Basic Education (or ABE) in the address.*

## Albuquerque TVI

Art Codova, dean
Montoya Campus
4700 Morris, NE
Albuquerque, NM 87111
505-224-5579

## Central Minimum Unit

William M. Jones,
  505-865-2770
Patricia Courtney,
  505-865-2732
3201 Highway 314 SW
Los Lunas, NM 87031

## Central New Mexico Correctional Facility

Carol Kovacs
PO Drawer 1328
Los Lunas, NM 87031
505-865-2363
f: 505-865-2316

## Clovis Community College

Zeke Martinez
417 Schepps Blvd
Clovis, NM 88101
505-769-4096

## CSB Correctional Center

Jane D. Wallen
PO Box 68
Fort Stanton, NM 88323
505-354-2250
f: 505-354-2534

## Dona Ana Branch Community College-NMSU

Donna Sewell
  505-527-7641
Debbie Bennett
  505-527-7544
30001/Dept 3DA
Las Cruces, NM 88003
3400 S. Espina St
Las Cruces, NM 88003
f: 505-527-7515
e-mail: nmsu/daccd.

## Eastern Navajo Agency

Mattie L. Bellinger and
  Paula M. Howard
PO Box 328
Crownpoint, NM 87313
505-786-6143/786-6149

## ENMU-Roswell

Avon Wilson
  505-624-7442
Judy Armstrong
  505-624-7276
  f: 505-624-7119
PO Box 6000
Roswell, NM 88202
58 University Blvd
Roswell, NM 88202

## ENMU-Ruidoso

Jim Miller
1400 Sudderth Drive
Ruidoso, NM 88345
505-257-2120
f: 505-257-9409

## Isleta Pueblo

Ulysses Abeita
PO Box 1270
Isleta, NM 87022
505-869-2597

## Mesa Technical College
*Jack Bryant, director*
824 West Hines
Tucumcari, NM 88401
505-461-4413
f: 505-461-1901

## Navajo Community College
*Lauren Bernally*
Box 580
Shiprock, NM 87420
505-368-5291 ext. 225

## New Mexico Junior College
*Marilyn Jackson*
5317 Lovington Highway
Hobbs, NM 88240
505-392-5411

## NMSU Alamogordo
*Anita Raynor and*
  *Joyce Reynolds*
PO Box 477
Alamogordo, NM 88210
505-437-5015

## NMSU Artesia Branch
*Jose Gallegos*
#8 Chalk Bluff Rd.
Artesia, NM 88210
505-746-2007(home)

## NMSU Carlsbad Branch
*Tino Abila*
*Pablo Martinez*
1500 University Drive
Carlsbad, NM 88220
505-885-6080
f: 505-885-6565

## NMSU–Grants
*Barbara Rawdon*
1500 N. Third St
Grants, NM 87020
505-287-7981 ext. 103
f: 505-287-2329

## Northern New Mexico Community College
*Lorenzo Gonzales*
1002 North Onate Street
Española, NM 87532
505-747-2197

## Santa Fe Community College
*Barbara Martinez*
PO Box 4187
Santa Fe, NM 87502
505-438-1643
f: 505-438-1237

## Socorro Consolidated Schools
*Jo Ann Salome*
PO Box 1157
Socorro, NM 87801
505-835-0300

## Southern New Mexico Correctional Facility
*Joe Curry*
PO Box 639
Jackrabbit Junction
Las Cruces, NM 88004
505-523-3271

## Southwestern Indian Polytechnic Institute
*Daisy Barney*
PO Box 10146
Albuquerque, NM 87184
505-897-5332

### Taos Educational Center (NNMCC)

*Olivia Martinez*
PO Box 3650
Taos, NM 87571
505-758-9369

### UNM–Los Alamos

*Jennifer McKerley*
4000 University Dr
Los Alamos, NM 87544
505-662-0338
f: 505-662-5919
e-mail: jgm@la.unm.edu

### Western New Mexico Correctional Facility

*Mary Ann Pauling*
PO Box 250
Grants, NM 87020
505-287-7961 ext. 312

### Western New Mexico University

*Toni Macias*
PO Box 680
Silver City, NM 88062
505-538-6310

### Women's Correctional Facility

*Dennis Cordova*
PO Box 800
Grants, NM 87020
505-287-2941 ext. 18

## OTHER LITERACY PROGRAMS

### Adult Education Center UNM Valencia Campus

*Pamela Etre-Perez*
280 La Entrada
Los Lunas, NM 87031
505-865-9598

### Adult Learning Center UNM–Gallup Campus

*Randy Larry*
200 College Rd.
Gallup, NM 87301
505-863-7525

### Albuquerque Literacy Program

*Cheri Downe, executive director*
1701 4th St SW
Albuquerque, NM 87102
505-768-6024

### Anthony Adult Learning Center DABCC-NMSU

*Cathy Concha and
 Celia Villalobos
Gadsden District*
Drawer 70
Anthony, NM 88021
505-882-3723

### Books for Babies New Mexico

*Dorothea Steinke*
 505-662-9362
*Joleen Frank*
 505-474-3940
PO Box 23138
Santa Fe, NM 87502

### Catholic Social Service

*Teresa Boyd*
PO Box 25405
Albuquerque, NM 87125
505-247-0442
f: 505-247-8335

### Chama Literacy Council

*Margaret Palmer*
299 4th Street
Chama, NM 87520
505-756-2388

## Clayton Literacy Council

*Janet Vialpando*
17 Chestnut Street
Clayton, NM 88415
505-374-9423

## Cochiti Community Library

*Lorencita Taylor and
   Amy Suina*
PO Box 153
Cochiti Pueblo, NM 87072
505-465-2885

## Crownpoint Institute of Technology

*Tommy Thompson*
PO Box 849
Crownpoint, NM 87313
505-786-5851 ext. 130

## Delancy Street / New Mexico, Inc.

*Peter Antinoro,
   education director*
PO Box 1240
San Juan Pueblo, NM 87566

## Deming Literacy Program

*Marie Sutter-Sinden*
PO Box 806
Deming, NM 88030
505-546-7279

## Eight Northern Indian Pueblos Council

*T.J. McReynolds*
PO Box 969
San Juan Pueblo, NM 87566
505-852-4265
f: 505-852-4835

## The Gathering Place

*Angela Bianco and Clara Begay*
PO Box 838
Thoreau, NM 87323
505-862-8075

## Hidalgo County Literacy Council

*Sydney Chilton*
500 E. 13th
Lordsburg, NM 88045
505-542-3529

## High School Equivalency Program (HEP)

*Dr. Frank Carrasco*
Northern New Mexico
   Community College
PO Box 26
El Rito, NM 87530
505-581-4139

## Home Education Livelihood Program (HELP)

*Albuquerque:*
*Ernest Ortega and
   Angel Fernandez*
5101 Copper, NE
Albuquerque, NM 87108
505-265-3717

*Clovis:*
*Rhonda Quails*
2505 Axtell
Clovis, NM 88101
505-7762-0045

*Española:*
*Mary Garcia*
800 La Joya
Española, NM 87532
505-753-7181

*more HELP next page…*

## Home Education Livelihood Program (HELP) • continued

**Las Vegas:**
PO Box 1247
Las Vegas, NM 87701
505-425-9307

**Mora:**
Ruth Fort
PO Box 541
Mora, NM 87732
505-387-2299

**Raton:**
Pam Jones
800 S. Second
Raton, NM 87740
505-445-9409

**Roswell:**
Mary Pasillas
100 N. Lea
Roswell, NM 88201
505-622-4460

## Jicarilla Apache Community Education Program

Loretta and Audrey Velarde
PO Box 306
Dulce, NM 87528
505-759-3708

## Laguna Pueblo Adult Education

Timothy Sarracino
PO Box 194
Laguna, NM 87026
505-552-6654 ext. 11
f: 505-552-6941

## Lea County Literacy Alliance

David Cook
New Mexico Junior College
5317 Lovington Highway
Hobbs, NM 88240
505-392-5411 ext. 547
f: 505-392-2527

## The Learning Assistance Center

Chuck Ridenour
New Mexico State
    University - Carlsbad
1500 University Drive
Carlsbad, NM 88220
505-885-8831 ext. 382,
505-885-4951

## Let's Read

Dauna Howerton
PO Box 62511
Española, NM 87532
717 Calle Don Diego
Española, NM 87532
505-753-9300
f: 505-753-6211

## Literacy Education Livelihood Program (HELP)

Mercedes Delgado
1252 Barker Road
Las Cruces, NM 88005
505-523-2411
f: 505-523-6646

## Literacy Program Penitentiary of New Mexico

Dr. Sheila Hyde
PO Box 27116, Highway 14
Santa Fe, NM 87502
505-827-8682
f: 505-827-8801

## Literacy Program Roswell Correctional Center

*John Analla*
578 W. Chicksaw Road
Hagerman, NM 88232
505-625-3121
f: 505-625-3190

## Literacy Volunteers of Socorro County
*Valerie Moore*
PO Box 1431
Socorro, NM 87801
505-835-4659
f: 505-835-1182

## Literacy Volunteers of Cibola County
*Shawn Barringer*
PO Box 306
Grants, NM 87020
505-285-5995

## Literacy Volunteers of Cimarron
*Ethel Ramsey*
PO Box 116
Cimarron, NM 87714
505-376-2305

## Literacy Volunteers of Dona Ana County
*Donna Sewell*
DABCC
Quintana Learning Center
PO 30001/Dept 3DA
Las Cruces, NM 88003
505-527-7641

## Literacy Volunteers of Santa Fe
*Letty Naranjo*
PO Box 4187
Santa Fe, NM 87502
505-438-1353

## Los Lunas Public Library
*Carmen Jaramillo*
460 Main St NE
Los Lunas, NM 87031
505-865-6779

## Luna Vocational-Technical Institute General Studies
PO Box K
Las Vegas, NM 87701
505-454-2570
f: 505-454-2518

## LVA-Carlsbad Literacy Program
*Ann Wood*
705 Elma Drive
Carlsbad, NM 88220
505-885-5068, 885-1752

## LVA-Grant County
*Orpha Gonzalez*
Western New Mexico
    University
PO Box 680
Silver City, NM 88062
505-538-6208
f: 505-538-6316

## LVA-Las Vegas/ San Miguel
*Christi Franken*
PO Box 819
Las Vegas, NM 87701
505-454-8043

## LVA-Otero County Literacy Council
*Joyce Reynolds*
New Mexico State University
Adult Basic Education
PO Box 477
Alamogordo, NM 88210
505-437-5015

## LVA-Raton
*Richard Azar, librarian*
224 Cook Ave
Raton, NM 87740
505-445-9711

## LVA-Valencia County Literacy Council
*Bolesio Lovato, Dolores*
*Hendricks and Dolores Padilla*
Belen Public Library
333 Becker Ave
Belen, NM 87002
505-864-7797
505-864-7522

## Mariano Lake Chapter House Literacy Program
*Raquel A. Warner*
PO Box 520
Gallup, NM 87305
505-786-5835

## NMSU-Carlsbad Language Retraining Program
*Ruth Anne Schnoor and*
*Suzanne Orrell*
1500 University Drive
Carlsbad, NM 88220
505-885-8831, 887-2658

## Project READ
*Gayle Dean*
203 West Main
Farmington, NM 87401
505-326-3503
f: 505-325-1688

## Ramah Navajo Continuing Education Program
*Yin-May Lee*
PO Box 160
Pine Hill, NM 87357
505-775-3253

## ReadWest-LVA
*Jeanette K. Miller*
PO Box 44508
Rio Rancho, NM 87174
505-892-1131

## Renewal Center San Juan College
*Marilyn Matthews*
4601 College Blvd
Farmington, NM 87401
505-326-3311 ext. 270

## Roosevelt County Literacy Council
*Mike Merchant*
1034 Community Way
Portales, NM 88130
505-356-8500

## Roswell Literacy Council
*Julie Wilcox and Lupe Bravo*
PO Box 2990
Roswell, NM 88201
505-625-1369
f: 505-623-0448

## San Felipe Pueblo Headstart/Literacy Program
*Edward Valencia*
PO Box A
San Felipe, NM 87001
505-867-2816

## Santa Fe SER Jobs for Progress
*Alex Martinez*
PO Box 2471
Santa Fe, NM 87504
505-473-0428
f: 505-438-4813

## SER de Albuquerque Jobs for Progress

*Pete Salazar, executive director*
*Lorie J. Barazno,*
  *program coordinator*
2118 Central Ave SE,
  Suite 33
Albuquerque, NM 87106
505-243-7717
f: 505-242-0627

*Also:*
*Gloria Aragon and*
  *Lisa Gonzales*
505-867-1537
f: 505-867-2792

## Shiprock Adult Education

*Roger Begay*
PO Box 3239
Shiprock, NM 87420
505-368-4427 ext. 385/386

## Sierra County Literacy Council

*Ellanie Sampson*
T or C Public Library
325 Library Lane
Truth or Consequences,
  NM 87901
505-894-3027, 894-7821
f: 505-894-2068

## Sunland Park Adult Learning Center (DABCC)

*Irene Aguirre and Rosa Sosa*
PO Box 1588
Sunland Park, NM 88063
505-589-1008

## Taos Literacy Program

*Carmen Medina*
114 Civic Plaza Dr.
Taos, NM 87571
505-758-8664
f: 505-758-7864

## Zuni Public Library Literacy Program

*Veronica Peynetsa*
PO Box 339
Zuni, NM 87327
505-782-5630

# Periodicals in New Mexico

 **D**aily and weekly newspapers are listed first, followed by a separate listing for magazines. The distinction is more difficult than it used to be. There are several monthly publications now turned out in a tabloid format on newsprint which could be either a newspaper or a magazine. (We have chosen to list all of these in the Magazine section.) Santa Fe is the home of the oldest continuously published daily newspaper (*The New Mexican*) and the oldest continuously published magazine (*El Palacio*) in the Southwest.

Where a publication regularly reviews books, we've included the name of the book editor or otherwise indicated a specific interest in books.

## NEWSPAPERS

### Albuquerque Journal
*Kent Walz, editor*
*David Steinberg, book editor*
7777 Jefferson NE
PO Drawer J, 87103
Albuquerque, NM 87109
505-823-3800
f: 505-823-3994

  Book reviews section edited by
David Steinberg.

### Albuquerque Tribune
*Scott Ware, editor*
*Ollie Reed, books reporter*
7777 Jefferson NE
Albuquerque, NM 87109
505-823-3600
f: 505-823-3689

### The Bulletin
*Stephen Klinger, editor*
1210 E. Madrid Ave
PO Box 637
Las Cruces, NM 88004
505-524-8061
f: 505-526-4621
e-mail: bulletin@zianet.com

### Cibola County Beacon
*J. D. Meisner, editor*
300 N. Second St
Grants, NM 87020
505-287-4411
f: 505-287-7822

### The Courier
*Gene Ballinger, editor*
Rio Valley Publishing
115 W. Hall St
Hatch, NM 87937
505-267-3546
f: 505-267-3019

### De Baca County News
*Scott Stinnet, editor*
412 Avenue C
Fort Sumner, NM 88119
505-355-2462
f: 505-355-7253

### Defensor Chieftain
*Gwen Roath, editor*
200 Winkler SW
Socorro, NM 87801
505-835-0520
f: 505-835-1837

### East Mountain Telegraph
*Charles Cantrell, publisher*
PO Box 710
Cedar Crest, NM 87008
505-281-2300
f: 505-281-2907

### El Hispano News
*A. B. Collado, publisher, editor*
El Hispano Publications
900 Park Ave SW
Albuquerque, NM 87103
505-243-6161
f: 505-842-5464

### Estancia Valley Citizen
*Morrow Hall, editor*
400 S. Fifth St
Estancia, NM 87016
505-384-2744

### Eunice Press
*Kent Brandley, editor*
PO Box 1095
Hobbs, NM 88241
505-394-3296
f: 915-586-2562

### Health City Sun
Alicia Alvarez, editor
PO Box 1517
900 Park Ave SW
Albuquerque, NM 87103
505-242-3010
f: 505-842-5464

### The Herald
Jim Streicher, editor
1204 N. Date
Truth or Consequences,
  NM 87901
505-894-2143
f: 505-894-7824

### Hobbs Daily News-Sun
Brenda Masengill, editor
PO Box 860
Hobbs, NM 88241
505-393-2123
f: 505-393-5724

### The Hobbs Flare
Rick McLaughlin, editor
114 E. Dunam St
Hobbs, NM 88241
505-393-5141
f: 505-393-1831

### The Independent
John K. Zollinger, publisher
PO Box 1210
Gallup, NM 87305
505-863-6811
f: 505-722-5750

### The Indian Trader
Bill Donovan, editor
311 E. Aztec
Gallup, NM 87301
505-722-6694
f: 505-863-6794

### The Jal Record
Velma Taylor, editor
PO Box Y
Jal, NM 88252
505-395-2516
f: 915-586-2562

### Las Cruces Sun-News
Jerry McCormack, editor
Las Cruces Newspapers, Inc.
PO Box 1749
Las Cruces, NM 88004
505-523-5481

### Lincoln County News
Ruth Hammond, editor
309 Central Ave
Carrizozo, NM 88301
505-648-2333

### Lordsburg Liberal
Jack Walz, publisher
PO Box L
Lordsburg, NM 88045
505-542-3471

### Los Alamos Monitor
Evelyn Vigil, editor
256 DP Road
Los Alamos, NM 87544
505-662-4185

Reviews books of local interest.

### Los Alamos Independent
Kenneth Van Riper, editor
PO Box 1347
Los Alamos, NM 87544
505-662-0805
f: 505-662-0761
e-mail:kvr@rt66.com

## The New Mexican

*Rob Dean, managing editor*
*Ruth Lopez, book editor*
202 E. Marcy St
Santa Fe, NM 87501
505-983-3303
f: 505-986-9147

Book review page every week.

## New Mexico Daily Lobo

*Dick Pfaff, publisher*
*Kandice A. McDonald, editor*
University of New Mexico
UNM Box 20
Albuquerque, NM 87131
505-277-5656
f: 505-277-6228

## The Observer

*Michael J. Ryan, editor*
1594 Sara Road SE
Rio Rancho, NM 87124
505-892-8080
f: 505-892-5719

## The Paper

*Chuck Pullins, publisher*
206-A W. Hill
Gallup, NM 87301
505-863-6753
f: 505-863-6736

## Quay County Sun

*Ron Wilmont, editor*
902 S. First St
Tucumcari, NM 88401
505-461-1952
f: 505-461-1965

## The Raton Range

*David Mullings, editor*
208 S. Third St
Raton, NM 87740
505-445-2721
f: 505-445-2723

## Rio Grande Sun

*Michael Kaemper, editor*
238 N. Railroad
Española, NM 87532
505-753-2126

## The Ruidoso News

*Joanna Dodder, editor*
104 Park Ave
Ruidoso, NM 88345
505-257-4001
f: 505-257-7053

## Sangre de Cristo Chronicle

*Ellen Goins, managing editor*
PO Drawer I
Angel Fire, NM 87710
505-377-2358

## Santa Fe Reporter

*Robert Mayer, editor*
PO Box 2306
Santa Fe, NM 87504
505-988-5541
f: 505-988-5348

Book review section.

## Santa Rosa News

*Darrel Freeman, publisher*
108 Fifth St
Santa Rosa, NM 88435
505-472-5454

## Sierra County Sentinel

*Bill Johnson, editor*
1747 E. Third St
Truth or Consequences, NM 87901
505-894-3088
f: 505-894-3998

## Silver City Daily Press

*Richard Correa, editor*
300 W. Market St
Silver City, NM 88061-0740
505-388-1576
f: 505-388-1196

## The Taos News

*Jess Williams, editor*
120 Camino de la Placita
Taos, NM 87571
505-758-2241
f: 505-758-9647

## Union County Leader

*Nick Payton, editor*
15 N. First St
Clayton, NM 88415
505-374-2587
f: 505-374-8117

## Valencia County News-Bulletin

*David Grenham, editor*
1837 Sosimo Padilla Blvd.
Belen, NM 87002
505-864-3549

## Weekly Alibi (formerly NuCity)

*Christopher Johnson, publisher*
*Michael Herrington, editor*
2118 Central Ave SE,
   Suite 151
Albuquerque, NM 87106
505-268-8111
f: 505-256-9651
e-mail: alibi@swep.com
web site:
   http://desert.net/alibi/

Reviews books regularly, contact Blake de Pastino.

# MAGAZINES

## The Abiquiu Post

*Richard Bock, publisher*
PO Box 69
Abiquiu, NM 87510

A publication of art, culture, local news and organic farming.

## The Adobe Journal

*Michael Moguin, publisher*
The Adobe Foundation
PO Box 7725
Albuquerque, NM 87194
505-243-7801
f: 505-243-7801

Quarterly; adobe architecture throughout the world.

## Albuquerque Woman

*Jill Duval, publisher*
*Susanne Dewitt, editor*
Duval Publications
PO Box 6133
Albuquerque, NM 87197
505-247-9195
f: 505-247-9129

Bimonthly; includes business, career issues.

## An Scéal

*Tierney Tully, editor*
PO Box 1076
Las Vegas, NM 87701
505-425-3390

Quarterly; news and features for the Irish, Scottish, Welsh, and Celtic communities of New Mexico.

## Book Talk

Carol A. Myers, *editor*
New Mexico Book League
8632 Horacio Pl NE
Albuquerque, NM 87111
505-299-8940
f: 505-294-8032

Published four times a year; Southwest information, book reviews, for booksellers, libraries, collectors ($15 per year). Some 500 subscribers in 44 states!

## Chile Pepper

*Robert Spiegel, publisher*
*Dave DeWitt, editor*
Out West Publishing
PO Box 80780
Albuquerque, NM 87198
505-266-8322
f: 505-266-2127

Bimonthly; spicy cuisine from around the world.

## Cowboys and Indians Magazine

*Charlotte Berney, editor*
128 Grant St
Santa Fe, NM 87501
505-989-3400
f: 505-989-3434

Bimonthly; western lifestyle.

## Crosswinds

*Steve Lawrence, editor*
*Dorothy Doyle, books editor*
3701 San Mateo Blvd. NE,
  Suite J
Albuquerque, NM 87110
505-883-4750, 986-0105
f: 505-883-4437

Monthly; news and views from New Mexico and abroad. Reviews books in every issue.

## El Palacio

Cheryle Mitchell,
  *managing editor*
PO Box 2087
Santa Fe, NM 87504
505-827-6451

Published three times a year; magazine of the Museum of New Mexico, and the oldest magazine in the Southwest. Reviews books about the region in every issue (art, anthropology, archaeology, history, culture, folk art).

## Enchantment

*Don Begley, editor*
*Marcia Muth, book editor*
New Mexico Rural Electric
  Cooperatives
614 Don Gaspar Ave
Santa Fe, NM 87501
505-982-4671
f: 505-982-0153

Monthly; for rural electrification consumers, includes reviews of New Mexico books in every issue.

## Frogpond: Quarterly Haiku Journal

*Elizabeth S. Lamb, editor*
The Haiku Society
  of America
970 Acequia Madre
Santa Fe, NM 87501
505-982-8890

Quarterly; contemporary English-language haiku, senryu, tanka, renga.

## Indian Artist Magazine
Michael Hice, editor
1807 Second St #61
Santa Fe, NM 87505
505-982-1600
f: 505-983-0790

Quarterly; contemporary Native
American arts.

## La Herencia del Norte
Ana Pacheco, publisher, editor
PO Box 22576
Santa Fe, NM 87502
505-474-2800
f: 505-474-2828

Quarterly; Hispanic past, present, and future.

## The Light
J. Bartholomew, publisher
PO Box 90611
Albuquerque, NM 87199
505-822-5010

Monthly; New Age, alternative

## Localflavor
Christopher Kolon,
  Janece Robertson, editors
223 N. Guadalupe #442
Santa Fe, NM 87501
505-988-7560
f: 505-988-9663
e-mail: flavor@rt66.com

Bimonthly; local food & wine
from ground to plate.

## Mothering Magazine
Peggy O'Mara, publisher, editor
PO Box 1690
Santa Fe, NM 87504
505-984-8116
f: 505-986-8335

Quarterly; progressive parenting.

## New Mexico Book View
Candelora Versace, editor
Jeanie Williams, managing editor
512 Acequia Madre
Santa Fe, NM 87501
505-988-3092
e-mail: candelora@aol.com
  cwabit1@aol.com

New monthly tabloid with
news about the New Mexico
literary community, book
reviews, author interviews, lists
of book events. Free circulation.
First issue: April 1997.

## New Mexico Business Journal
Robert J. Cochnar,
  editor & publisher
Sierra Publishing Group
420 Central SW
Albuquerque, NM 87102
505-243-3444
f: 505-243-4118

Monthly; business.

## New Mexico Historical Review
Robert Himmerich y Valencia,
  editor
University of New Mexico
1013 Mesa Vista Hall
Albuquerque, NM 87131
505-277-5839
f: 505-277-6023

Quarterly; historical essays, documents.

## New Mexico Magazine

*Emily Drabanski, editor*
*John Bowman, books editor*
State of New Mexico
Lew Wallace Building
495 Old Santa Fe Trail
Santa Fe, NM 87503
505-827-7447
f: 505-827-6496

Monthly; New Mexico travel and history; Southwestern cuisine. Southwest bookshelf in every issue.

## New Mexico Wildlife

*Jeffrey L. Pederson, editor*
NM Dept. of Game and Fish
Villagra Building
PO Box 25112
Santa Fe, NM 87504
505-827-7917
f: 505-827-7915

Bimonthly; wildlife, conservation.

## Outside

*Lawrence J. Burke, publisher*
*Mark Bryant, editor*
Mariah Publications Corp.
Outside Plaza, 400 Market
Santa Fe, NM 87501
505-989-7100
f: 505-989-4700

Monthly; outdoor sports; related travel, environmental issues.

## The Perspective

*Tom Kelly, publisher, editor*
Cheallaigh Shamrock
PO Box 815
Las Cruces, NM 88004
505-522-7744
f: 505-521-7315

Biweekly; business in the Southwest.

## Prime Time

*Arthur Alpert, editor*
PO Box 7104
Albuquerque, NM 87194
505-880-0470
f: 505-888-1450

The Monthly for New Mexicans 50+. Monthly book reviews; books of local interest.

## Quote

*Tom Kelly, publisher, editor*
Cheallaigh Shamrock
PO Box 815
Las Cruces, NM 88004
505-522-7744
f: 505-521-7315

Monthly; material for public speakers.

## Royal City News

*Rosemary Zibert, editor*
1807 Second St, #65
Santa Fe, NM 87505
505-982-3526
e-mail:
    webworks@roadrunner.com
web site:
    http://www.rcnews.com

On-line magazine for and about Santa Fe; photos and features.

## The Santa Fean Magazine

*Manya Winsted, publisher,*
*Lesley King, managing editor*
The Santa Fean Magazine and
    Publishing Co.
1440-A St Francis Drive
Santa Fe, NM 87501
505-983-8914
f: 505-983-8013

Published eleven times a year; Santa Fe history, events, personalities.

### Santa Fe Business

*Martin L. Gerber,*
*publisher & editor*
PO Box 88
Santa Fe, NM 87504
f: 505-982-3058

Weekly; news and opinions that impact local businesses.

### Santa Fe Kids!

*Alexis Sabin, publisher, editor*
515 Don Gaspar
Santa Fe, NM 87501
505-471-7773
f: 505-474-3440

Quarterly; activities and events for children.

### The Santa Fe Sun

*Shawn & Betty Townsend,*
*publishers, editors*
2074 Galisteo, A5
PO Box 23168
Santa Fe, NM 87502
505-989-8381
f: 505-989-4767
e-mail: sfsunnm@aol.com

Monthly; alternative, spiritual. Bookshelf review column.

### Site Architecture

*Ronald Christ, editor*
40 Camino Cielo
Santa Fe, NM 87501
505-988-5820
f: 505-988-9236
e-mail: site@rt66.com

On-line magazine for architecture.

### Southwest Profile

*John K. Whitney, publisher;*
*Stephen Parks, editor*
Whitney Publishing Co.
PO Box 1236
Santa Fe, NM 87504-1236
505-989-7603

Quarterly; Southwest art, architecture, style.

### Stereophile

*Larry Archibald, publisher*
*John Atkinson, editor*
PO Box 5529
Santa Fe, NM 87502
505-982-2366
f: 505-983-6327

Monthly; high-end audio equipment; music reviews.

### Stereophile Guide to Home Theater

*Larry Archibald, publisher*
*Lawrence E. Ullman, editor*
PO Box 5529
Santa Fe, NM 87502
505-982-2366
f: 505-983-6327

Quarterly; home theater equipment, laserdisc reviews.

### Tantra: The Magazine

*Alan Verdegraal, publisher*
*Susana Andrews, editor*
PO Box 79
Torreon, NM 87061-0079
505-384-2292

Quarterly; tantric practices, history.

## Taos Magazine

*John K. Whitney, publisher*
Whitney Publishing Co, Inc.
PO Box 1380
Taos, NM 87571
505-758-5404

## THE magazine

*Guy Cross, Judith Wolf,*
  *publishers, editors*
520 Franklin Ave
Santa Fe, NM 87501
505-982-5785
f: 505-983-7649
e-mail: THEmag1@aol.com

Published eleven times a year;
New Mexico arts, events.

## Tradición Revista

*Barbe Awalt & Paul Rhetts,*
  *publishers, editors*
LPD Enterprises
2400 Rio Grande Blvd, NW
  #1213
Albuquerque, NM 87104
505-344-9382
f: 505-345-5129
e-mail: paullpd@aol.com

The journal of contemporary
and traditional Spanish Colonial
art and culture.

## Women's Voices

*Louisa Dyer*
PO Box 40572
Albuquerque, NM 87196
505-294-7788
e-mail: cybergrrlz@aol.com

Monthly; a Southwest feminist
journal of thoughts, arts and
events.

## The Workbook

*Kathy Cone, editor*
Southwest Research &
  Information Center
PO Box 4524
Albuquerque, NM 87106
505-262-1862
f: 505-262-1864

Quarterly; review journal of the
alternative press.

## Tumbleweeds

*Claudette E. Sutton, editor*
369 Montezuma #191
Santa Fe, NM 87501
505-984-3171
f: 505-984-3171
e-mail: tumbleweeds@sfol.com

Quarterly; for northern New
Mexico families and people who
work with children.

# Printers & Binders

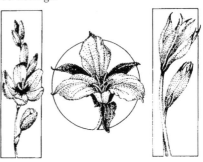

**W**hile there are many general and specialty printers in New Mexico, only a few are capable of trade hardcover and paper-bound book printing, and even fewer are competitive with national book printers. To our knowledge, just Starline and Guynes, and possibly Albuquerque Printing, are able to produce a standard trade book completely in-house. There are no four-color web presses in New Mexico, and even *New Mexico Magazine* is printed out-of-state. One reason is that there are no commercial paper mills nearby (a mixed blessing). A word of caution: some firms in both this section and the **PUBLISHING SERVICES** section may advertise themselves as book printers, yet will have many parts of a job (such as binding, film lamination, and in some cases even the printing itself) farmed out to suppliers. For best control over the quality of your job, always ask what procedures a printer may have to send to other contractors.

New Mexico firms that do various types of bookbinding are listed next under **Bookbinders**.

Most trade book publishers in the state depend on dedicated book printers in the Midwest and South. The owners or sales reps of a number of the most reliable ones are NMBA members, and these are listed under **Book Printers Outside New Mexico** following the New Mexico listings.

## NEW MEXICO PRINTERS

## ALBUQUERQUE

### Academy Printers
4740 Pan American Fwy. NE
Albuquerque, NM 87107
505-884-1737

### Adobe Press Inc.
*Glenda Dawson*
515 Isleta Blvd SW
Albuquerque, NM 87105
505-873-1155
f: 505-873-9766

### Aiken Printing
1112 Third NW
Albuquerque, NM 87102
505-243-5631

### Alameda Printing
*Dick Moots*
9128 4th St NW
Albuquerque, NM 87114
505-898-0880

### Albuquerque Printing
*Tony Fernandez*
5514 Coal SE
Albuquerque, NM 87108
505-265-8831
f: 505-255-7857

### Alphagraphics
*See Publishing Services.*

### Aspen Printing Co., Inc
*Len Baggerman*
2517 Comanche NE
Albuquerque, NM 87107
505-880-0002
f: 505-880-8338

### Century Printing, Inc.
*Walt Kearus*
3300 Princeton NE, Ste N7
Albuquerque, NM 87107
505-884-6454

### Cooper Press
*Scott Cooper*
2430 Juan Tabo NE
Albuquerque, NM 87112
505-296-5446
f: 505-296-3175

### Cottonwood Printing
2117 Osuna Place NE
Albuquerque, NM 87111
505-345-5341

### Dataco, Inc.
1712 Lomas NE
Albuquerque, NM
505-243-2841

### First Impression, Inc.,
*Terry Buster*
8320 Lomas NE
Albuquerque, NM 87110
505-255-6321
f: 505-255-7639

### Gordon Printing Co.
*Sally Blackstad*
712 5th St NW
Albuquerque, NM 87102
505-252-4303

### Graphic Solutions Inc.
*Gene Scanlon*
2414 San Mateo Pl NE
Albuquerque, NM 87110
505-880-0383
f: 505-880-1381

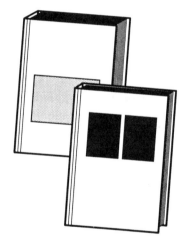

## Guynes Printing

*Stan Anglen*
2709 Girard NE
Albuquerque, NM 87107
505-884-8882
f: 505-884-0079

## High Country Printing & Graphics

*Vince Mouser*
2415-K Princeton NE
Albuquerque, NM 87107
505-888-7994
f: 505-881-3284

## Intermountain Color

*Kevin Neff*
4701 Lincoln Road NE
Albuquerque, NM 87109
505-884-9703
f: 505-884-1684

## Lithexcel

*Waleed Ashoo*
2408 Alamo SE
Albuquerque, NM 87106
505-243-8560
f: 505-243-8579

## The McLeod Co., Inc.

*Gene Wintermute*
1516 5th St NW
Albuquerque, NM 87102
505-243-1714
f: 505-243-1702

## The New Valiant

*Robert Cody*
615 Gold SW
Albuquerque, NM 87102
505-247-4175
f: 505-246-8891

## P E R Printing

*Thomas C. Foulk*
1216 San Pedro NE
Albuquerque, NM 87110
505-254-9672
f: 505-254-9769

## Pop Printing, Inc.

*Heights*
*George Ortiz*
10900 Menaul NE,
   Suites C & D
Albuquerque, NM 87110
505-298-9009
f: 505-298-9009

*Midtown*
4501 Bogan NE
Albuquerque, NM 87109
505-881-6666

## Printer's Press

*Peter Renna*
5505 Lomas NE
Albuquerque, NM 87110
505-268-7659

## Quick Print

*Uptown*
*Mike Moore*
5000-E Menaul NE
Albuquerque, NM 87110
505-881-2927

*Downtown*
20 First Plaza, Ste. 209
Albuquerque, NM 87102
505-247-0334

## Richard's Printing

*David Nadolny*
719 San Mateo NE
Albuquerque, NM 87108
505-256-7735
f: 505-256-7739

## The Sherwood Co.
7615 Menaul NE
Albuquerque, NM 87110
505-292-5900

## Starline Printing
William P. Lang
7111 Pan American Hwy NE
Albuquerque, NM 87109
505-345-8900
f: 505-344-9763

## Universal Printing
1224 Bellamah NW
Albuquerque, NM 87104
505-842-8820

## BOSQUE FARMS

### Boughman's Print-N-Copy
Carol Butler
1155 Bosque Farms Blvd
Bosque Farms, NM 87068
505-869-6060
f: 505-869-4235

## CARLSBAD

### Myers Printing Inc.
Ralph Leyva
111 N Alameda Street
Carlsbad, NM 88220
505-885-3665
f: 505-885-0293

### Nichols Printing
Gary Lanier
212 W. Lea
PO Box 608
Carlsbad, NM 88220
505-885-3313
f: 505-885-6449

## CLAYTON

### Jobe's Press
Debbie McCord
113 Main Street
Clayton, NM 88415
505-374-9436
f: 505-374-2452

## ESPAÑOLA

### New Mexico Office Products
Marlo R. Martinez
216 N Riverside Drive
Española, NM 87532
505-753-7271
f: 505-753-7700

## FARMINGTON

### Accent Copy Service
Fred Willmon
214 S. Court
Farmington, NM 87401
505-326-1344

### The Reprographics Center
Ralph Pugmire
814 W. Apache
Farmington, NM 87401
505-326-2269
f: 505-326-3336

### San Juan Reproduction
Chuck Kahwajy,
  Danny Carpenter
135 Airport Dr
Farmington, NM 87401
505-327-5044
f: 505-327-5046

## HOBBS

### Hobbs Printing Co.
*Rudy Rascon*
305 W. Broadway
Hobbs, NM 88240
505-393-2335
f: 505-393-2335

### Superior Printing
*Ray David Little*
517 E. Broadway
Hobbs, NM 88240
505-393-3261, 397-1236
f: 505-393-3261

## LAS CRUCES

### ABC Printing Co. Inc.
*Larry Martin, Lois Martin*
406 N. Downtown Mall
Las Cruces, NM 88001
505-526-9283, 526-5575
f: 505-527-0509

### ASAP Printing Centers
820 E. Lohman Avenue
Las Cruces, NM 88001
505-523-8661
f: 505-523-8662

### Del Valle
925 South Walnut
Las Cruces, NM 88001
505-526-6101
f: 505-525-9119

### Intermountain Color
*Micah Gove*
132 Westgate, Suite A
Las Cruces, NM 88005
505-525-9675
f: 505-525-9681

### RB Design & Printing
2391 N. Mesquite
Las Cruces, NM 88001
505-523-1704
f: 505-523-1708

## LOS LUNAS

### Flyer Press
*Ellen Syvertson*
59 Highway 49
Los Lunas, NM 87031
505-865-6365
f: 505-865-6365

## MILAN

### Cibola Printing
*Ron Armstrong*
PO Box 3372, 720 Route 66
Milan, NM 87021
505-285-4361
f: 505-285-6530

## PORTALES

### Graphic Works
*Berwin Howard*
208 S. Main Ave
Portales, NM 88130
505-356-2824

## RIO RANCHO

### Dry Land Press
*Eddie Williams*
1030 Veranda Dr, SE
Rio Rancho, NM 87124
505-892-3637

## Rio Rancho Printing

*Audra Dodson*
408 Frontage Road
Rio Rancho, NM 87124
505-892-8553
f: 505-892-1196

## ROSWELL

### Alpha-Omega Printing

*K. Denise Rawdon*
211 W. Third Street
Roswell, NM 88201
505-624-2700
f: 505-624-2733

## RUIDOSO

### Ruidoso Printing

*Scott Muhn*
1713 Sudderth Dr
Ruidoso, NM 88345
505-257-2325
f: 505-257-2199

## SANTA FE

### Alphagraphics

2002 C Cerrillos Rd
Santa Fe, NM 87501
505-473-1300
f: 505-473-3460

### Blue Feather Press

2884 Trades West Rd
Santa Fe, NM 87501
505-471-7519

### Cloud Bridge

825 Early St
Santa Fe, NM 87501
505-983-6763

### Copygraphics

314 Read St
Santa Fe, NM 87501
505-988-1438

### Easy Print

1426 Cerillos rd
Santa Fe, NM 87501
505-988-3456

### General Printing

150 Aggie Rd
Santa Fe, NM 87502
505-471-2992

### Mariposa Printing

922 Baca
Santa Fe, NM 87501
505-988-5582

### Ortiz Printing

*Ralph Ortiz*
1519 Third St
Santa Fe, NM 87505
505-983-4271
f: 505-983-9495

### Piñon Fast Printers

*Bryan Brigham*
950 Cordova
Santa Fe, NM 87501
505-982-1777

### Roller Design / Printing Services

*Albert Scharf*
320 Sandoval
Santa Fe, NM 87501
505-983-5858
f: 505-988-3122

## Santa Fe Printing
*Norma & Carl Evans*
1424 Second St
Santa Fe, NM 87501
505-982-8111
f: 505-984-8133

## Schifani Brothers Printing
502 Cerrillos Rd
Santa Fe, NM 87501
505-982-0812

## SPRINGER

### The Tribune Press
*Carlos Gutierrez*
405 Third St
Springer, NM 87747
505-483-2222

## TAOS

### Columbine Printing, Inc.
*John D. Batis*
201 Camino De la Merced
Taos, NM 87571
505-758-8486, 800-816-8486
f: 505-758-3714

### Deckerhoff's Printers
*Phil Omerod, Uvaldo Jeantete*
622F Paseo del Pueblo Sur
Taos, NM 87571
505-758-8638
f: 505-758-8639

## BOOK PRINTERS OUTSIDE NEW MEXICO (with NMBA Members)

### Braun-Brumfield Inc.
*Robert E. Ryan*
100 North Stuebler Rd
Ann Arbor, MI 48103
313-662-3241
f: 313-662-1667

Complete short to medium run book manufacturing; disk-to-film capability; perfect and notch binding and case binding.

### Data Reproductions
*Al Kelly*
1480 N. Rochester Road
Rochester Hills, MI 48307
810-652-7600
f: 810-652-7605
datarep@ibm.pat

Trade book printer providing all binding styles; one and two color text from camera-ready copy or disk; four color covers.

### Gilliland Printing, Inc.
*Becky Allison*
215 N. Summit
Arkansas City, KS 67005
800-332-8200, 316-442-0500
f: 316-442-8504

Specializes in perfectbound book runs from 500 to 20,000, with 10-20 day turnaround times and disk-to-film capabilities.

## McNaughton & Gunn

*Ron Mazzola*
960 Woodland Drive
Saline, MI 48176
313-429-5411
f: 800-677-BOOK

Complete book printing for perfectbound and case binding; competitive for runs from 250 copies to 25,000.

## Patterson Printing

*Linda Seaman, sales rep*
1550 Territorial Road
Benton Harbor, MI 49022
800-848-8826, 616-925-2177
f: 616-925-6057

Full service book printer for high quality short and long runs; complete bindery and competitive pricing.

## Ripon Community Printers

*Alex Goulder*
1919 Fourteenth St, #540
Boulder CO 80302
303-443-7884
f: 303-443-8288
e-mail: goulder@earthnet.net

High-quality, low-cost softcover book printer; non-heatset web presses; complete digital prepress services.

## Rose Printing Co.

*Charles Rosenberg, president*
Rob Covello, sales rep
2503 Jackson Bluff Road
Tallahassee, FL 30304
800-227-3725
f: 904-576-4153
e-mail: rose@freenet.fsu.edu

Short run (250-5000) book manufacturer with in-house bindery for both perfectbound

and case binding; specialize in minibooks and lay-flat binding.

## Thompson-Shore, Inc.

*Jim Holefka, Kay Stevens*
7300 West Joy Road
Dexter, MI 48130
313-426-3939
f: 800-706-4545
e-mail: http://www.tshore.com

Major short and medium run trade book printer with complete bindery and state-of-the-art electronic prepress capability.

## Vaughan Printing Inc.

*David Prentice, sales rep*
411 Cowan Street
Nashville, TN 37207
615-256-2244
615-259-4576

State-of-the-art electronic prepress capabilities in one to four colors; short to medium runs of from 500-10,000 books.

## Walsworth Publishing

*Dave Plumer, sales rep*
306 N. Kansas Avenue
Marceline, MO 64658
800-369-2646 ext. 5721
f: 816-258-7798

Quality short-run sheet-fed book printer, specializing in four-color and halftone reproduction; casebound and softcover books.

## BOOKBINDERS

### Bookbinders of New Mexico Inc.

2521 Comanche Rd NE
Albuquerque, NM 87107
505-881-1178

### Bullet Bindery

3600 Osuna Rd NE
Albuquerque, NM 87109
505-343-0176

### Esperanza Bookbindery

2276 Don Felipe Rd SW
Albuquerque, NM 87105
505-873-1750

### Plastikoil of the Southwest

3100-E Pan American Frwy
   NE, Bldg. #2
Albuquerque, NM 87107
505-888-1787

### Summit Trade Bindery

2720 Vassar NE
Albuquerque, NM 87107
505-884-8142

### Sunray Trade Bindery

2520 San Mateo Blvd. NE
Albuquerque, NM 87110
505-884-3838, 884-3150
f: 505-888-1944

# Publishing Services

These are firms and individuals who serve New Mexico's publishing industry in a variety of ways—from people who edit and design books, to those who do typesetting and provide color separations, to marketing and publicity experts. Because of the computer revolution, coming up with appropriate categories isn't as easy as it used to be. Today's designer may also do typesetting and pre-production work; roles are changing almost daily. "Desktop publishing" (a misnomer to begin with) usually means getting finished pages, on paper or on disk, ready for the printer.

The section is organized into four categories: (1) **Design, Prepress and Graphic Services**; (2) **Editors and Indexers**; (3) **Literary Agents**; and (4) **Marketing and Publicity**. Design, Prepress, and Graphics Services includes general service bureaus, traditional typesetters, laser scanning, film output, PMTs, layout, and other technical and professional wonders. Not every shop does every operation; we suggest you call to find out the current specialties and capabilities of each. (🗲 indicates a firm owned or operated by a NMBA member.)

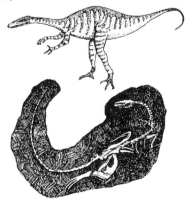

## DESIGN, PREPRESS & GRAPHIC SERVICES

### A-1 Signs by Leo
608 Pinon Dr
Santa Fe, NM 87501
505-983-2261

### A-Hill Design Ltd.
112 Edith Blvd NE
Albuquerque, NM 87102
505-242-8300

### Tony Abeyta Arts & Graphics
901 W San Mateo Rd
Santa Fe, NM 87501
505-820-0523

### AD Design Inc.
901 San Mateo, Suite J
Santa Fe, NM 87501
505-989-3739

### ADD Design
1432 Jefferson St NE
Albuquerque, NM 87110
505-344-3696

### Alphagraphics
1930-A Juan Tabo NE
Albuquerque, NM 87112
505-275-1642

1730 Lomas NE
Albuquerque, NM 87106
505-243-1842

8202-A Menaul NE
Albuquerque, NM 87110
505-292-4149

9500 Montgomery NE
Albuquerque, NM 87110
505-292-4149

3700 Osuna NE, Ste 505
Albuquerque, NM 87109
505- 344-8797

3771 Southern Ave
Albuquerque, NM 87107
505-892-5156

4001 San Mateo NE
Albuquerque, NM 87110
505-883-0752

1400 17th St,
Los Alamos, NM 87544
505-662-7881

2082 C Cerrillos Rd
Santa Fe, NM 87501
505-473-1300

### ✺ An Extra Hand
*Nancy Hewitt*
627 Gomez Rd
Santa Fe, NM 87501
505-989-4119

### Arnold Litho
5908 Lomas Blvd NE
Albuquerque, NM 87110
505-266-4371
f: 505-266-9798
m: 505-266-2289

### The Art Center
2268 Wyoming Blvd NE
Albuquerque, NM 87112
505-298-1828

### ASAP Printing Centers
820 E Lohman Ave
Las Cruces, NM 88001
505-523-8661

## Atomic Dog-Graphic Design

418 Cerrillos Rd
Santa Fe, NM 87501
505-986-0077

## Bear Canyon Creative

6753 Academy Rd NE
Albuquerque, NM 87109
505-823-9150

## Bruno Design Associates

128 Grant
Santa Fe, NM 87501
505-982-5544

## ❧ Buffalo Publications

*Gene Crouch*
718 Baca
Santa Fe, NM 87501
505-983-1226

## Burning Books

*Michael Sumner*
PO Box 2638
Santa Fe, NM 87504
505-820-6216
f: 505-820-6216
e-mail: brnbx@nets.com

## Business Graphics Inc.

3314 Vassar Dr NE
Albuquerque, NM 87107
505-884-2244
f: 505-884-1668

## Busy BEE's Typing

Las Cruces, NM 88001
505-523-7660

## Camera Ready Productions

1231 Southbridge Dr
Las Cruces, NM 88001
505-526-2755
f: 505-526-3227

## Cisneros Design

1516-A Pacheco St
Santa Fe, NM 87501
505-983-6677

## ❧ John Cole

*Graphic Designer*
3 Juego Pl
Santa Fe, NM 87505
505-466-7311

## Conception Graphic Design

710 13th NW
Albuquerque, NM
505-242-9094

## ❧ Connor Design

*Julie Connor*
223 N. Guadalupe
Santa Fe, NM 87501
505-982-7895
f: 505-982-0908
e-mail:
    dzinmuz@unix.nets.com

## Cook Design

PO Box 6049
Santa Fe, NM 87502
505-466-1310
505-989-9570

## Cooper Press

2430 Juan Tabo NE
Albuquerque, NM 87112
505-296-5446

**Copygraphics**
314 Read St
Santa Fe, NM 87501
505-988-1438
f: 505-988-3155

**Creative Imagery**
*Yvonne Walston*
3640 High St NE
Albuquerque NM 87107
505-344-8986
f: 505-344-8986

**Dancing Fool Creations**
213 Los Pinos, La Cienega
Santa Fe, NM 87501
505-474-4444

**Desk Top Publishing**
*John Gravel*
418 Cerrillos Rd
Santa Fe, NM 87501
505-982-0588

**Design Associates, Inc.**
1117 Landman NE
Albuquerque, NM 87112
505-299-9216

**Design Synergy**
369 Montezuma St
Santa Fe, NM 87501
505-986-1215

**DesignLine Sasha Pyle**
1672 Cerro Gordo Rd
Santa Fe, NM 87501
505-988-5388

**Don Mickey Designs**
3904-B Central SE
Albuquerque, NM 87108
505-256-7031

**David R Faulkner Associates**
6209 Academy Ridge Dr
Albuquerque, NM 87111
505-296-5944

**The Front Office Inc.**
1323-C Paseo de Peralta
Santa Fe, NM 87501
505-986-5800

**Judy Gale of Sombrillo**
Espanola, NM
505-753-3885

**Gecko Graphics**
2415 Princeton Dr NE
Albuquerque, NM 87107
505-881-3098

**General Printing Service**
150 Aggie Road
Santa Fe, NM 87505
505-471-2992

**Geo-Graphics Lettering & Design**
3300 Princeton Dr NE, S4
Albuquerque, NM 87104
505-883-0500

**Get Type & Graphics**
1540 Cerrillos Rd
Santa Fe, NM 87501
505-988-2040
f: 505-984-1849

**Gianopoulos Design**
6417 Torreon Dr NE
Albuquerque, NM
505-823-9048

## Graphics Galore Inc.
2403 San Mateo Blvd NE
Albuquerque, NM
505-884-7577

## Marilyn Hager Design
76 Moya Rd, El Dorado
Santa Fe, NM 87505
505-466-3720

## Hayduk-King Advertising
1219 Luisa St
Santa Fe, NM 87501
505-988-9299

## ❧ H. Margret Studio
*Margret Henkels*
622-C Canyon Road
Santa Fe, NM 87501
505-989-8032

## IN ICTV OCVLI
1712 Callejon Emilia
Santa Fe, NM 87501
505-982-7977

## Insty-Prints
1907 Saint Michaels Dr
Santa Fe, NM 87505
505-982-0122

## Intermountain Color
132 Westgate
Las Cruces, NM 88001
505-525-9675

## JB Accurate Die
*Dies, embossing & foil stamping*
3300 Princeton Dr NE
Albuquerque, NM 87107
505-889-0428

## Louann Jordan
*Graphic Designer*
1524 Camino Sierra Vista
Santa Fe, NM 87501
505-983-2994

## C Kensman Design
718 Mountain Rd NW
Albuquerque, NM 87102
505-242-9207

## Kilmer & Kilmer, Inc.
152 Truman NE, Suite 200
Albuquerque, NM 87108
505-260-1175

## Kinko's Copies
*New Mexico locations*
2706 Central Ave SE
Albuquerque, NM 87104
505-255-9673

2400 Louisiana Blvd NE
Albuquerque, NM 87110
505-881-5383, 875-2000

2520 Juan Tabo NE
Albuquerque, NM 87112
505-291-9300

6220 San Mateo NE
Albuquerque, NM 87109
505-881-2222

1713 E. University Ave
Las Cruces, NM 88001
505-522-5758

*More Kinko's next page…*

513 Montezuma
Santa Fe, NM 87501
505-982-6311

730 St. Michaels Dr
Santa Fe, NM 87505
505-473-7303

**John Knox Design**
137 E. Santa Fe Ave
Santa Fe, NM 87501
505-982-1896

**Kokopelli Design**
129 W San Francisco, Suite A
Santa Fe, NM 87501
505-986-1776

**L V B Design**
834 Griegos Rd NW, #2
Albuquerque, NM 87107
505-345-7447

**Letter Press Services**
*Dies, embossing & foil stamping*
1239-C Bellmah NW
Albuquerque, NM 87104
505-242-0650
f: 505-843-7946

**Lizarraga & Ruiz**
Albuquerque, NM
505-281-8161

**Macnab Design**
400 San Felipe NW
Albuquerque, NM 87104
505-242-6159

**ﻉﻉ Jim Mafchir**
*Publications & Graphic Services*
126 Candelario St
Santa Fe, NM 87501
505-988-7214

 **Meaders Secretarial**
330 Garfield
Santa Fe, NM 87501
505-986-6065

**MetroGlyph**
2917 Carlisle Blvd NE
Suite 107
Albuquerque, NM 87110
505-888-4005

**Michael Motley Studio**
320 Aztec
Santa Fe, NM 87501
505-982-0355

**Mousepad Imaging**
4111 Louisiana Blvd NE
Albuquerque, NM 87109
505-880-1540

**Mulhern & Company
Advertising Inc.**
4147 Montgomery Blvd NE
Albuquerque, NM 87109
505-884-1005

**Bill Murphy**
*Covers & Book Design*
486 Circle Dr
Santa Fe, NM 87501
505-983-9607

## Murray's Design
3217 Silver Ave SE
Albuquerque, NM 87106
505-268-8865

## New Grub Street Graphic Design
*Deborah Mrantz, designer*
129 Del Rio Dr
Santa Fe, NM 87501
505-984-0716

## Nightingale Hice
544 S. Guadalupe
Santa Fe, NM 87501
505-982-1600

## Nobul Graphics
4401 Montgomery Blvd NE,
   Suite 5A
Albuquerque, NM 87109
505-889-9769

## OnLine Design
9353 Guadalupe Trail NW
Albuquerque, NM 87114
505-898-5711

## ੈ Jaye Oliver
*Illustrations*
1600-B Brae Street
Santa Fe, NM 87505
505-820-7092

## Paper Tiger
*Design Graphics &*
   *Color Separation*
1248 San Felipe Ave
Santa Fe, NM 87505
505-983-3101
f: 505-986-6033
e-mail:
   lannisl@ix.netcom.com
web: http://users.aol.com/
   lannisl/tigerwww/

*Branch:*
*Paul Kelly*
120 E Marcy St
Santa Fe, NM 87501
505-983-2839

## The Printmaker Ltd.
1807 Second St, Suite 40
Santa Fe, NM 87505
505-983-5666
f: 505-983-0847
m: 505-983-0857

## Peters & Co.
*Graphic Designs*
PO Box 90502
Albuquerque, NM 87119
505-898-2386

## Prairie Tale Design Studio
418 Cerrillos Rd
Santa Fe, NM 87501
505- 984-0234

## E J Predika Studio
Moriarty, NM
505-832-6141

JAYE OLIVER
ILLUSTRATION
· DESIGN ·
505·820·7092

SANTA FE GRAPHIC DESIGNS

DESIGN
ILLUSTRATION
COMPUTER GRAPHICS

*B*ARBARA A. *M*YERS

PO Box 2507 • Santa Fe, NM 87504
Phone 505: 466-4636 • Fax: 505 466-9788
e-mail bamyers@roadrunner.com

## Rainbow Color & Prepress
*Tony Isaacs, owner*
PO Box 472
Taos, NM 87571
800-748-1540, 505-776-2763
f: 505-776-2804

## Rapid Copy Center
3515 Wyoming Blvd NE
Albuquerque, NM 87111
505-296-6555

## Reece Graphics Ltd.
2129 Osuna Rd NE, #111
Albuquerque, NM 87113
505-345-2004

## Rick Johnson & Co. Inc.
1120 Pennsylvania NE
Albuquerque, NM 87110
505-266-1100

## Roller Design/ Printing Services
320 Sandoval
Santa Fe, NM 87501
505-474-5858

## Rt. 66 Design Inc.
4487 Irving Blvd NW
Albuquerque, NM
505-897-9957

## Janice St. Marie
*Illustrator*
1101 Don Diego Ave
Santa Fe, NM
505-988-1872

## Sandhill Studios
*John Crane*
Santa Fe, NM 87501
505-988-5282

## ❧ Santa Fe Graphic Design
*Barbara Myers*
PO Box 2507
Santa Fe, NM 87504
505-466-4636
f: 505-466-9788
e-mail:
    bamyers@roadrunner.com

## The Sharky Group
*Mary Lambert*
301 Gold Ave, SW
Albuquerque, NM 87102
505-843-6696

## 602 Marketing Group
418 Montezuma, Suite D
Santa Fe, NM 87501
505-986-9602

## Sloves Products
*Book Packaging*
5101 Copper Ave NE
Albuquerque, NM 87108
505-255-2552

## SOS (Graphic Services)
204 N Guadalupe
Santa Fe, NM 87501
505-983-6306

## Southwest Electronic Prepress Services
3812 Academy Pkwy
    North NE
Albuquerque, NM 87109
800-955-7714, 505-345-7714

## ❧ Sovereignty Press

*Production Services*
*Sara Benjamin-Rhodes*
PO Box 6095
Santa Fe, NM 87502
505-466-6975
f: 505-466-0887
e-mail:
  sovpress@internetMCI.com

## ❧ Sterling Publishing Services

*Evalyn Schoppet*
12404 Chelwood Trail NE
Albuquerque, NM 87112
505-271-2866
f: 505-271-2866

## Subia-The Image Makers

6612 Gulton Ct NE
Albuquerque, NM 87109
505-345-2636
f: 505-344-9177

## Sun Graphics Design

3330 Candelaria Rd NE
Albuquerque, NM 87107
505-884-2080

## ❧ Mary Sundstrom Illustrations

*Mary Sundstrom*
1909 Kriss Place, NE
Albuquerque, NM 87112
505-294-0582

Editing, typography,
graphics & design
*Sovereignty Press*
(505) 466-6975

## ❧ Sunstone Press

*James Clois Smith Jr.*
239 Johnson St
Santa Fe, NM 87501
505-988-4418

## Mary Sweitzer Design

425 Kathryn Pl
Santa Fe, NM 87501
505-988-8042

## Swisa Design

1609 Don Gaspar Ave
Santa Fe, NM 87501
505-988-4818

## Tech Reps, Inc.

5000 Marble Ave NE
Albuquerque, NM 87104
505-266-5678

## Trade Printing Inc.

*Mike Woerner*
3434A Vassar NE
Albuquerque, NM 87107
505-883-4214
f: 505-889-0520

## Tru Colour Inc.

3825 Osuna Rd NE
Albuquerque, NM 87109
505-343-4002

**MARY SUNDSTROM**
Illustrator
(505) 294-0582

## Vaughan / Wedeen Creative Inc.

407 Rio Grande Blvd NW
Albuquerque, NM 87104
505-243-4000

### ∂ Webworks

*Web page development & design*
Bernadette Sanchez
1807 Second St, #65
Santa Fe, NM 87505
505-982-3526
e-mail:
  webworks@roadrunner.com

### ∂ White Hart Design

*Kathleen Sparkes*
1803½ Alvarado NE
Albuquerque, NM 87110
505-268-3534

## William Field Design

355 E Palace Ave
Santa Fe, NM 87501
505-988-8888

## Ken Wilson Design Inc.

5504 Moon NE
Albuquerque, NM 87111
505-823-0181

## Your Thoughts

1422 McCurdy Circle
Espanola, NM 87532
800-780-8231
505-753-8231

# EDITORS & INDEXERS

## American Society of Indexers

*Francine Cronshaw,*
  *NM contact: 505-281-8422*
PO Box 48267
Seattle, WA 98148
206-241-9196
f: 206-727-6430
e-mail: asi@well.com

### ∂ Agee Indexing Services

*Victoria Agee*
7436 El Morro Rd, NE
Albuquerque, NM 87109
505-823-2306
keeg55c@aol.com

### ∂ Nancy S. Avedisian

*A+ Productions*
PO Box 2444
Santa Fe, NM 87504
505-988-4434
f: 505-989-1030

book design
typography • illustration
advertising
**Kathleen Sparkes**
505/268-3534

**EDITING SERVICES**
Nancy Avedisian
(505)988-4434
*Relentless devotion to the written word*

### ᵃᵂ Jenifer Blakemore

809 Gonzales Road
Santa Fe, NM 87501
505-820-0800

### ᵃᵂ Blessingway Author Services

*Ellen Kleiner*
134 E. Lupita Road
Santa Fe, NM 87505
505-983-2649
f: 505-983-2005

### Bea Bragg

1800 Glorieta NE, Apt 1
Albuquerque, NM 87112
505-294-0148
bscribe@aol.com

### Margaret E. (Peggy) Durbin

1526-A 43rd Street
Los Alamos, NM 87544
w: 505-665-3364
h: 505-662-0694
f: 505-665-3750

### ᵃᵂ East Mountain Editing Services

*Francine Cronshaw*
PO Box 1895
Tijeras, NM 87059
505-281-8422
f: 505-281-8422
cronshaw@unm.edu

### Sally Gwylan

8821 Central NW., #3
Albuquerque, NM 87121
505-836-3396

### ᵃᵂ Mary Dungan Megalli

PO Box 1375
El Prado, NM 87529
505-751-1184

### ᵃᵂ Sovereignty Press

*Production Services*
*Sara Benjamin-Rhodes*
PO Box 6095
Santa Fe, NM 87502
505-466-6975
f: 505-466-0887
e-mail:
    sovpress@internetMCI.com

### ᵃᵂ Sterling Publishing Services

*Evalyn Schoppet*
12404 Chelwood Trail NE
Albuquerque, NM 87112
505-271-2866

### Marylee A. Thomson

704 Columbia St
Santa Fe, NM 87505
w: 505-983-0737
h: 505-988-3616
f: 505-988-3616
mat@santafe.edu

### ᵃᵂ Elizabeth Wolf

*Editor*
1013 Camino de Chelly
Santa Fe, NM 87505
505-982-4078

## LITERARY AGENTS

### Irene W. Kraas

220 Copper Trail
Santa Fe, NM 87505
505-474-6212
f: 505-474-6216

### ❧ Mary Luders
*Literary Agent*
434 Acequia Madre
Santa Fe, NM 87501
505-982-5302

### Luna Court Literary Agency
*Robert Covelli*
544 E Coronado Rd
Santa Fe, NM
505-983-4788

### Rydal Agency
*Clark Kimball*
PO Box 2247
Santa Fe, NM 87504
505-983-1680

## MARKETING SERVICES

### Action Point Image
14 Monterey Rd
Santa Fe, NM 87501
505-466-0903

### Blanchard-Bedford Inc.
13 Calle Alejandra
Santa Fe, NM 87501
505-466-7063

### The Front Office Inc.
1323-C Paseo De Peralta
Santa Fe, NM
505-986-5800

### Ha-Lo Marketing & Promotions
*Michael Madanick*
Santa Fe, NM 87501
505-822-1803

### Hine & Stock Associates
1226 Galisteo
Santa Fe, NM 87501
505-989-1933

### ❧ Keeler Communication
*Edy Keeler*
89 Apache Ridge
Santa Fe, NM 87505
505-466-4040
f: 505-466-8223

### ❧ Margaret Klee Lichtenberg & Associates
*Maggie Lichtenberg*
23 Monterey Rd
Santa Fe, NM 87(505) 8288
505-466-1616
f: 505-466-3802
margaretkl@aol.com

### Marketing Counselors International
825 Calle Meja
Santa Fe, NM 87501
505-982-9792

---

**MARGARET KLEE LICHTENBERG**

Marketing Coach

voice 505-986-8807
fax 505-986-8794
email margaretkl@aol.com

P.O. Box 268
Santa Fe, NM 87504

---

### Robert T Ritter Companies

612 Old Santa Fe Trail
Santa Fe, NM 87501
505-984-3006

### Southwest Planning & Marketing

903 W Alameda, #206
Santa Fe, NM 87501
505-989-8500

### West Coast Group

*Marketing & Sales Consultants*
Santa Fe, NM 87501
505-983-9400

### Special Use Products

County Road 0020
Espanola, NM 87532
505-747-1323

### Focus First America Field Management Inc.

826 Camino del Monte Rey
Santa Fe, NM 87501
505-982-7520

### Quick Test

4250 Cerrillos Rd
Santa Fe, NM 87501
505-471-1699

### Research & Polling Inc.

*Brian Sanderoff*
7500 Jefferson NE, Suite 250
Albuquerque, NM 87109
505-821-5454

### Southwest Planning & Marketing

903 W Alameda #206
Santa Fe, NM 87501
505-989-8500

# Illustrations

**15** Jaye Oliver, from *Welcome Home*
by Sandra Ingerman, published by Harper Collins

**35** John D. Rice Jr., from *From Santa Fe to O'Keeffe Country:*
*A One-Day Journey Through the Soul of New Mexico,*
by Rhoda Barkan & Peter Sinclaire, Ocean Tree Books, 1996

**48** Claiborne O'Conner, from *Ceaser of Santa Fe,*
by Tim MacCurdy, Amador Press, 1990

**53** John D. Rice Jr., from *From Santa Fe to O'Keeffe Country:*
*A One-Day Journey Through the Soul of New Mexico*

**79** Jaye Oliver, from *Soul Retrieval*
by Sandra Ingerman, published by Harper Collins

**82** Jaye Oliver, unpublished

**97** Claiborne O'Conner, from *Souls and Selves Remembered,*
by Harry Willson, Amador Press, 1987

**106** John D. Rice Jr., from *From Santa Fe to O'Keeffe Country:*
*A One-Day Journey Through the Soul of New Mexico*

**116** Jaye Oliver, printed in J. F. Kennedy University catalog

**127** John D. Rice Jr., from *From Santa Fe to O'Keeffe Country:*
*A One-Day Journey Through the Soul of New Mexico*

# Join the Book People of New Mexico!

**W**e are passionate book people who have come together through our common interests to preserve, protect, and promote the *Book* in all its forms. We are book readers, book professionals, publishers, illustrators, writers, librarians, designers, typesetters, printers, service bureau providers, literacy advocates, magazine people, distributors, book packagers, marketing and publicity people, and reviewers. We're expanding rapidly and we invite all who are interested in the books arts and profession to join us.

You will receive the monthly *Libro* newsletter, filled with useful information for New Mexico's book people, and opportunities to take part in our other programs and cooperative activities, including our monthly networking luncheons and dinners.

**YES!** I'd like to join the NMBA! Enclosed with this form is $50 for my membership and up to 35 words of description of my business or professional activity for inclusion in *New Mexico's Book World* resource guide and *Libro* newsletter:

Your Name: _____

Business / Institution: _____

Address: _____

City _____ State _____ Zip _____

Phone_____ Fax _____

E-Mail _____

Description of business or activity:_____

_____

_____

_____

_____

**Send to: New Mexico Book Association**
**PO Box 1295 • Santa Fe, NM 87504**
**505-983-1412**